The Danger Zone
Lost in the Growth Transition

By

Jerry L. Mills, CPA

Library of Congress Cataloging-in-Publication Data
is available upon request.

ISBN 0-615-13318-5

First Edition, June 2006

Second Edition, September 2007

Dedication

Entrepreneurs and risk-takers of the world

Acknowledgements

Jack A. Henry

Larry Checketts

Christine, Natalie, Dale, Nathan

and Stephanie Mills

Prelude

Nothing in the world can take the place of persistence. Talent will not; nothing is more common than unsuccessful individuals with talent. Genius will not; unrewarded genius is almost a proverb. Education will not; the world is full of educated derelicts. Persistence and determination alone are omnipotent.[1]
- Calvin Coolidge, 30th U.S. President

All achievements, whether in the business, intellectual, or spiritual world, are the result of definitely directed thought, are governed by the same law and are of the same method; the only difference lies in the *object of attainment*.

He who would accomplish little must sacrifice little. He who would achieve much must sacrifice much. He who would attain highly must sacrifice greatly. [2]
- James Allen

Contents

Dear Business Owner:

This is an open letter to the risk-takers of our society - the owners of closely held growth companies. You are the reason our economic society works. You employ the largest number of salaried employees in our country.

You feel the truthfulness of the adage, *"It is lonely at the top."* You sometimes wonder if anyone will ever understand you, your goals, your business wishes and ambitions. You also have frustrations that cause you to worry about your business. Some of these worries are with you 24/7, 365.

Many of your peers have expressed sentiments to me such as, *"I do not understand why I had more cash when my company was much smaller than it is today;" "I do not understand why bankers will not give me the money I need;" "I used to love my business when I first started, but now I feel trapped;" "I don't have time to leave the office to spend time with customers or my family;"* and so forth.

Expressions similar to the above are symptoms of a larger problem, a phenomenon I call **The Danger Zone**. The purpose of this book is to help you understand this phenomenon and to give you some suggestions to avoid or get out of this situation.

The goal of this book will have been accomplished if it helps one business owner avoid or escape from The Danger Zone. Hopefully, it will help many.

Jerry L. Mills

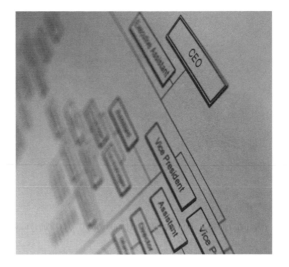

CHAPTER 1

The Unofficial Organization of Your Company

I'd like to start this book by sharing some information that I have learned from decades of working with the owners of closely held companies. You will not learn the following information from college. Your understanding of this information will assist you greatly in the future as your company grows.

Some authors have attempted to explain this subject, but none have done so in the concise manner that you will see in this book. I have explained this subject matter in a practical way by departing from some of the idealistic methods found in other books.

The learned professors who write popular books will tell you that you need two things to be successful in your company, (1) a mission statement and (2) an organization chart. It's difficult to argue the logic of these PhDs and learned people, but I am going against their grain with this book because of the goal stated in my letter to you, which is to help you avoid The Danger Zone (TDZ).

Mission Statements

When I began this business back in 1987, I assumed that I would need to help my clients document a mission statement. That was, after all, what the learned professors had told me to do in their popular business books. Well, I quickly found that trying to get a business owner to create a mission statement was harder to do than to get one of my teenagers to clean up his or her bedroom.

I am a fan of well-written mission statements. There is nothing wrong with the logic of a mission statement, but such statements typically do not work for the owners of closely held companies. There are a variety of reasons why they do not work; the major reason is business owners feel confined or constrained by the mission statement.

Why would a mission statement be confining to a business owner?

The answer to that question is business owners are very creative. They thrive on change. They also like control and do not appreciate others trying to force them into a position they do not want to take. Boxing a business owner into a corner with something such as a mission statement is unwise and counter-productive.

People looking from the outside of a closely-held business tend to judge the business owner by the look and feel of the "main" business without understanding that the business owner either has, or is in the process of creating other businesses, some of which the public may not see very often. Most non-entrepreneurs do not understand that the true entrepreneur needs to create other businesses, some of which may not relate at all to the primary business that is visible to the community.

An outside consultant might spend days helping a business owner create a mission statement. The consultant will then charge a lot of money and say, *"The job is done."*

Well, the job is not done because the mission statement most likely will not fit the other business or businesses the entrepreneur is going to create. In fact, the mission statement may conflict with the other businesses or the future vision the owner has of the company. The new mission statement is then viewed as confining and unnecessary to the business owner. Too often, the mission statement becomes an impediment to the entrepreneur.

B2B truism: *Mission statements are sometimes interesting but are not critical to a company's success.*

I am not alone in my philosophy that creating a mission statement is not a critical "end" step in running or creating a company. One of my favorite books states:

"Creating a (mission) statement can be a helpful *step* in building a visionary company, but is only one of thousands of steps in a never-ending process."[3]

Core Values or Mission Statements?

Entrepreneurs may have a better chance of improving their business by defining core values than they do by writing mission statements. *Permanent core values should outlast mission statements.* Core values of a business are like the foundation of a building that has the ability to have other stories or rooms added to the building without changing the foundation.

Core values can be defined as:

"The organization's essential and enduring tenets – a small set of general guiding principles; not to be confused with specific cultural or operational practices; not to be compromised for financial gain or short-term expediency."[4]

Some core values that we often see are:

- Honesty and ethics
- Hard work
- Integrity
- Superior customer service
- Constant improvement to the company

What Are the Right Core Values?

There is not a list of core values that will fit into your organization. Rather, core values must come from your inner-most beliefs and desires. Core values are not a marketing position statement that will shift with the tide. The experts on this subject have said:

"When articulating and codifying core ideology, the key step is to capture what is authentically believed, not what other companies set as their values or what the outside world thinks the ideology should be.

"In a visionary company, the core values need no rational or external justification. Nor do they sway with the trends and the fads of the day. Nor even do they shift in response to changing market conditions.

"Visionary companies tend to have only a few core values, usually between three and six. In fact, we found none of the visionary companies to have more than six core values, and most have less. And, indeed, we should expect this, for only a few values can be truly *core* – values so fundamental and deeply held that they will change or be compromised seldom, if ever."[5]

Display Your Core Values

I have lived long enough to have learned that you can't teach core values in a business environment. People are either honest or they are not. They most likely learned this honesty or dishonesty before age five and there is nothing you can to do to change their core values.

People either have good work ethics or they are lazy. People desire either to improve the company or have a desire to undermine the company.

B2B truism: *You can't teach values but you can find people who share your core values.*

You might consider writing down the *three to six* core values that you wish for your company. Post this list in visible places in your business, perhaps even on your website. You can now begin to hire people (employees, attorneys, accountants, bankers, etc) who share your core values.

It is no accident that the core values of B2B CFO® are listed on the home page of my firm's website at www.b2bcfo.com.

Hold On to Your Core Values

Core values should not shift with the tides
of change in a business, as evidenced by the
following words of wisdom:

"Enduring great companies preserve their
core values and purpose while their business
strategies and operating practices endlessly
adapt to a changing world. This is the magical
combination of 'preserve the core and stimulate
progress.' "[6]

Employee Skills vs. Core Values

Should a business owner hire a skilled person
even if this person does not share the core values
of the company or the owner?

This is a tough subject for business owners. I
have seen business owners hire people because
they have a special skill, even if they know
the person does not share their values. This is
a mistake for those companies that have core
values:

"Myth: Visionary companies are great places to
work, for everyone."

"Only those who 'fit' extremely well with the core ideology and demanding standards of a visionary company will find it a great place to work. If you go to work for a visionary company, (i.e., a company that establishes core values and core ideologies) you will either fit and flourish – probably couldn't be happier – or you will likely be expunged like a virus. It's binary. There's not a middle ground. It's almost cult-like. Visionary companies are so clear about what they stand for and what they're trying to achieve that they simply don't have room for those unwilling or unable to fit their exacting standards."[7]

There is a different way to look at this concept. Have you ever been in a situation where you were wearing dirty clothes and then accidentally found yourself with a group of people who were well dressed? If you have not been in this situation, then imagine how you would feel. Of course, you would most definitely feel out-of-place. You would feel self-conscious and would try to get away from that group of people as soon as possible.

And so it goes with core values. Let's say you have a core value of honesty. You hire people who are honest. This honesty is not only in their heart, but is a part of their being. These people enjoy working with others who share this philosophy.

Let's imagine you then hire a person who is not honest. What is going to happen in this situation? The outcome is predictable: the honest people will feel uncomfortable around the dishonest person. Things will be said behind this person's back such as, *"Why do you think the owner hired him?"* The dishonest person will try to fit in, but the other employees won't allow this to happen. They may not say anything to the boss (a job security issue), but they will not socialize or trust this person. It would be easier to try to mix water and oil.

B2B truism: *You want to get rid of anyone in your organization who does not share your core values. You also want those people to be hired by your competition. You will smile and consider it a victory when your competitor hires your former associates or employees who do not share your core values, regardless of their skills.*

Let's create a situation about core values, simply as an example. Imagine that you adopt one of the core ideologies of Motorola:

"Treat each employee with dignity, as an individual."[8]

This sounds easy, doesn't it? What qualities would a company need to have to treat each employee with dignity? A few words come to mind: fairness, calmness, composure, self-control, restraint, kindness, wisdom, etc.

Let's select just one word from the preceding list, *calmness*.

What does it take to treat employees (or others) with calmness? What are the rewards that follow a person who achieves calmness in personal dealings with others in business relationships? James Allen wrote the following words about this subject in the early 1900's in one of my all-time favorite books, *As a Man Thinketh:*

"The calm man, having learned how to govern himself, knows how to adapt himself to others; and they, in turn, reverence his spiritual strength, and feel that they can learn of him and rely upon him. The more tranquil a man becomes, the greater his success, his influence, his power for good. Even the ordinary trader will find his business prosperity increase as he develops a greater self-control and equanimity, for people will always prefer to deal with a man whose demeanor is strongly equitable."[9]

What are your core values? What are the core values of your company? **Document these values.** Good core values are a type of a mission statement!

Why Organization Charts Do Not Work

Let's look at another subject in which I got my knuckles rapped many times before I learned a tough lesson.

It took me about a decade to figure out why owners of closely-held companies do not like organization charts. This was frustrating to me! In many instances I felt I had failed my clients. After all, the experts who write popular books preach that a company needs to have such a document to succeed.

I tried in vain to follow that advice. After many failures I have concluded that owners of closely held companies will not be forced to use an organization chart, regardless of the number of times I implore them to use one. I have given up on the matter. By giving up, I have learned to listen to my clients and to find better ways to help communicate with them on the organization of their companies.

There are numerous reasons business owners do not like organization charts, a few being:

(1) They fear that managers and supervisors will ask for pay raises if they see they are on an "equal level" with other managers or supervisors on the chart.

(2) The organization of the company is constantly changing which gives the owner a moving target at all times.

(3) Business owners are good at delegating responsibility but bad at delegating authority, thus the chart is rendered useless.

B2B truism: *If you delegate responsibility without the authority, you will after a period of time, be given back the responsibility.*

(4) Business owners like to talk to employees within the boundaries of a horizontal organization chart instead of the typical organization chart.

(5) The business owners fear that some employees will not perform duties that are not included in the organization chart. The fear is that an employee might say, "That is not my responsibility."

(6) The organization chart does not typically allow consideration of other entities that might be smaller than the largest entity.

(7) Overall, it is a confining document to the business owner.

Now, do not hear what I am *not* saying. I am not saying that I condone horizontal delegation of duties. Conversely, I strongly believe in the process of delegation of authority and responsibility through managers and supervisors.

On the other hand, the business belongs to the business owner. The owner has the *right* to talk to anyone in the company, regardless of a formal chain of command. Anyone who disagrees should volunteer to the business owner to start writing payroll checks out of his or her own personal account.

I will discuss the topic of delegating responsibility *and* authority in a subsequent chapter. For now, we can safely conclude that the typical organization chart will not work for the owner of a closely-held company. There is, however, a very simple alternative to creating a formal organization chart that does not take much effort to document. The beauty of the following is that *everyone* in your company will understand it immediately and will not argue its logic or challenge its disciple.

The Unofficial Organization Chart

Each company owned by an entrepreneur has an unofficial organization chart. The future success of the company is predicated upon how well this organization chart functions. The unofficial organization chart looks like the following:

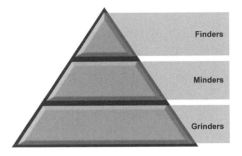

B2B truism: *Whether written or unwritten, the company's organization chart exists today. The Finder's future success is dependent upon working properly within the rules of the informal organization chart.*

I will discuss the roles of *Finders, Minders and Grinders* [10] in the following chapters. I'd like to emphasize before we get into some of the detail that, as a business owner, it is very important for you, the Finder, to understand this informal organization of your company. The key to making this organization chart work is the Finder. The organization will function well if the Finder does his or her duties properly. The organization will fail if the Finder does not perform as needed.

The organization chart of the company that is headed for The Danger Zone looks like the following:

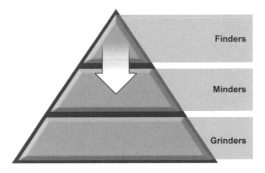

The objective of this book is to do the following with the above organization chart:

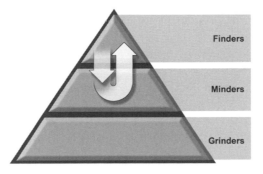

The next chapter discusses the roles of Finders.

CHAPTER 2

Entrepreneurs are Finders

I have been working with business owners since I graduated from Arizona State University in 1978. I have asked them hundreds of questions to try to figure out their logic and thought processes. More importantly, I have observed their decision making and their reactions to both the extreme good and the extreme bad. I have learned from them and want to share with you some of the important things I have learned.

They Are Different

It is important to understand that entrepreneurs are different from everyone else in our society.

They typically have an above-average IQ, even though most of them are reluctant to admit such a fact. I had the opportunity to work with a particular client for many years who had only a high school education and was embarrassed to admit that fact to others. Yet he is one of the most intelligent people I have ever met. He has a high IQ, regardless of the fact that he does not have a post-secondary education.

Entrepreneurs usually have high ethical and moral business core values. Most of them are very creative.

Contrary to myth, most of them don't do what they do "just for the money." Contrary to another myth, they typically care deeply about their employees and associates. Their heart often aches with the personal tragedies of their employees, although many entrepreneurs do not always openly show their feelings.

It Is Lonely at the Top

Entrepreneurs live in the future and have the attributes to take the risk to do something about the future. They will risk their money, time and their fortunes to make a difference in the future.

The future is all that matters to entrepreneurs!

This is one of the key differences between them and others in our society. While the employees may have fleeting thoughts about their future, they functionally live their lives in either the past or the present.

One thing that often frustrates entrepreneurs is the realization that they are alone in the organization in their concerns regarding the future of their company. This is one of the reasons for the adage, *"It is lonely at the top."* It truly is a lonely spot, but it is really the only place to be for those of us who are entrepreneurs. This fact makes it possible for us to take advantage of opportunities.

Entrepreneurs need to realize that, with few exceptions, nobody will ever really understand or empathize with that loneliness.

B2B truism: *It is lonely at the top. Don't expect anyone to understand or empathize with that loneliness.*

They Pull People Into the Future

Entrepreneurs spend a significant amount of time and energy *pulling* people into the future. They will hold meetings and retreats, write memos, write e-mails, and use other methods, to try to express their visions and ideas. In frustration, they will sometimes say, *"Does anyone ever listen?"*

Well, the answer is *yes* they will listen, but they will *not* understand. They may understand a part of the vision, but they will never understand the "big picture" that you have in your mind. They do not understand risk. They do not understand the need entrepreneurs have to create and to succeed.

Life Time Zones

The employees, and most people with whom the entrepreneur is surrounded, live in different time zones than does the entrepreneur. This doesn't mean Mountain Standard Time (MST) vs. Eastern Standard Time (EST). I refer here to "life time zones" that are just as different as MST vs. EST, and are easy to distinguish, once entrepreneurs understand the concept of life time zones within individuals.

Knowledge is power. It is important for the entrepreneur to understand this concept. The terminology I use is:

Life Time Zone	Common Reference	B2B Reference
Future	Entrepreneur	Finder
Past	Managers or Administration	Minder
Present	Technicians or Laborer	Grinder

The remainder of this book will refer to entrepreneurs and business owners as *Finders,* which is a more accurate description of their function within the organization. I will also go into some detail on Minders and Grinders in an effort to help Finders avoid *The Danger Zone.*

Finders are very different from Minders and Grinders. We can thank our Maker that they were born that way; otherwise, the future of economic society would be very bleak.

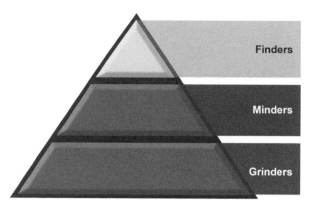

CHAPTER 3

Finders Live in the Future

This chapter will explain some of the basic concepts of the role of the Finder in the company organization.

Finders are the leaders of the company. They are not necessarily the people who lead all company employees on a daily basis. Finders demonstrate the type of leadership that "pulls" people into the future - employees, current customers and future customers.

B2B truism: *Finders live in the future with little regard to what has happened in the past.*

Let's identify who is *not* a Finder. A sales person, a company's sales force and the people who manufacture the widgets are not Finders. These people are grinders, which is discussed in a subsequent chapter.

Finders demonstrate some specific attributes that are essential to this success. There are numerous terms that can describe the leadership of a Finder; the following few will give you the main idea.

- Visionary
- Idea generator
- Innovator or dreamer
- Catalyst for future change
- Relationship builder or creator

You will notice that all of the above attributes or functions require "future" action. Hence, Finders are all about the future. They do not live in the past. They view the past as a tool from which to learn, not as a place in which to dwell.

This concept of the "future" thinking of Finders took me many years to understand. The first time this came to my attention was when I was working in public accounting in the 1980s. Our clients would pay significant amounts of money for audits and other types of services that were mostly historical in nature. I found it odd that the Finders would spend so much money for these services but show so little interest in what we were doing. Finally, in frustration, I gathered enough courage to ask a Finder why he was not interested in what my colleagues and I were doing. *"After all,"* I said, *"you are paying a lot of money for this information."* He looked at me and quietly said, *"Jerry, at this moment I am very worried about making my next payroll."* He then looked away from me and totally ignored me. That was a significant moment in my learning about Finders.

As I sat there in front of this good man, I pondered what he might do if he could not pay his people at the time of the next payday. Suddenly, my concerns about what I felt was important to this Finder seemed trivial. I had a job to do for my employer, but I realized that as a professional, I had not yet developed the proper insight concerning the needs of my Finder clients.

That experience instilled in me a desire to learn so that I could eventually help Finders with whatever concerns they might have, especially if it were making the next payroll for their employees.

The Beginning Is All About Finding

Finders start their business or businesses in countless ways. In the beginning there is one constant. The Finder spends most of his or her time in "finding activities," which typically give the Finder an adrenalin rush. They will work six or seven days a week, often for long periods of time, to be involved in these finding activities, which include:

- Building relationships with customers
- Creating relationships with vendors
- Delegating tasks to employees or associates
- Causing sales and cash to come into the company

Mostly Relationship Building

The above activities have one thing in common: they all are mostly about the Finder creating relationships with others.

A good Finder spends most of his or her time building relationships and "pulling" others into the Finder's future. The success of any company is due to the relationships that the Finder is able to make with others. *Building relationships takes time* and is typically the best time the Finder can spend in helping the company succeed. Show me a good Finder who will spend 30 to 40 hours a week in finding activities and I will show you a company that will have significant increases in sales in the future. Conversely, show me a Finder who stops spending time in finding activities and I will show you a company that is starting the inevitable cycle of getting into financial trouble.

B2B truism: *Successful Finders are good relationship builders.*

As a Finder, you need to understand *minding* and *grinding* in order to avoid being caught up in the activities of minding and grinding. In the next chapters we are going to spend some time talking about those activities and what they entail.

B2B truism: *Finders evoke strong emotions from others, such as love or hate. There is no reason to try to be friends with everyone, because they are looking for a leader, not a friend.*

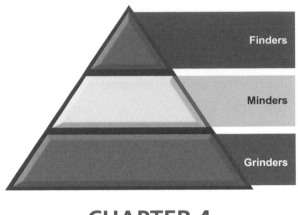

CHAPTER 4

Minders Live in the Past

Minders are critical to the company's success: the company will not survive without good Minders. I work with good Minders every day and have learned to appreciate both their intelligence and their desire to help the Finder. Most Minders are very loyal to their boss. They are typically very honest and ethical in their business dealings.

Minders are the key administrative people of the company. A Minder may be the company's controller, bookkeeper, finance manager, CFO, IT Director, IT Manager, etc.

Minding is good and minding activities are necessary for the success of any company.

Therefore, hiring, training and retaining good Minders is critical for the future success of any company.

B2B truism: *Minders live in the past and are not future-thinkers.*

Most of the assignments given to Minders deal with historical matters or events that have happened in the past, such as:

- Last month's sales tax return
- Historical financial statements
- Last month's bank reconciliation
- Filing documents
- Making copies of information for bankers
- Fixing a computer that crashed
- Installing software and converting old data

All of the above items are important to be done and to be done correctly. Finders simply need to be aware that it is often difficult for Minders to be concerned about something that might happen a year or two in the future when they are working overtime to try to finish documenting things that have been done in the past. It is hard for the mind to be in two different time zones at the same time.

B2B truism: *Finders are not good Minders.*

Finders typically do not have the accounting, IT or other background to work extensively in minding activities. By nature, Finders detest this work. They resent the fact that they have to spend their time in countless meetings, working on cash flow, hiring and firing people, meeting with accountants, attorneys, bankers, etc.

Common Mistakes

Finders often unintentionally make mistakes in their relationships with their Minders. Some of these mistakes are a result of the Finder not understanding the life time zone difference between a Finder and a Minder. Finders often like to simply sit and ramble for long periods of time with the Minder about the future of the company and other things. The Finder does not always understand that, while interested, the Minder is worried about the extra amount of time it will take to get back to work and finish the things that need to be done.

Minders need to be led by the Finder or by others. There is nothing wrong with the need to be led; it is the natural order of things in a business.

Minders are very practical and logical. They do not like *rah-rah* leading from Finders. They like facts. They do not like to be told a story they can't believe.

Below are some ideas that will help you with your relationship with your Minders:

- Meet on a regular basis with your Minders to establish the priorities. Ask them what they are working on and what they feel are their priorities for the next few weeks. Listen. You may not always understand why they have certain priorities. If this is the case, ask why they have set these priorities. Express why you may agree or disagree with the priorities. It is always best to have the Finder and the Minder agree on priorities.

- Minders do not have the same intestinal fortitude as do Finders about tight cash situations. There is nothing wrong with this and a Finder should not expect a Minder to enjoy going to work each day in a company that does not have cash to pay its bills. Meet often with your Minder if the company's cash is tight.

Explain in detail your plan to correct the cash situation. If you do not have a plan, make one by going out and finding the right people to correct the situation. Do not expect the Minder to fix your company's cash flow problems.

- As a company grows, the Minder is often put in a situation where he or she simply does not understand what to do in many accounting or IT situations. As the Finder, be the leader and get a mentor to help teach the Minder. Don't expect a miracle from the Minder if the person simply has not been taught how to take care of all of the situations of a growth company.

- Finders often create more than one company. Levels of complexity are introduced when multiple companies owned by the Finder start doing business together, such as sales, transfers of cash, payments of loans, etc. These transactions, called *intercompany transactions*, are often very complicated and often have implications to the Finder in business, banking and taxation circumstances. It is not wise to assume your Minder will understand how to deal with all of these situations. In these situations a Finder should get a mentor for the Minder.

- Minders are motivated by the Finder sincerely showing appreciation for work well done. A showing of appreciation, such as a gift certificate for two at a nice restaurant, will go a long way to show a sincere appreciation for work well done.

- Do not ask your Minder to be a check signer on business accounts. As will be discussed in a later chapter, you are placing this person in a situation to fail.

Minders are critical to your company. As a Finder, realize that your role will most likely be less of a *skills* teacher and more of a *leader* to your Minders.

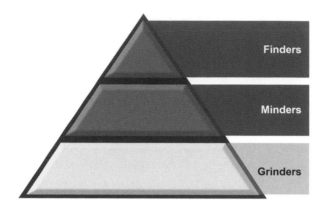

CHAPTER 5

Grinders - Today is all that Matters

B2B truism: *Most Finders started their careers as Grinders.*

"Most successful business owners had some knowledge or experience with their chosen industry before they ever opened their own businesses." [11]

Grinders are people who do the physical work of the company. In a manufacturing company, the Grinder is the person who makes the widgets. The Grinders are the people doing the construction work in a construction company. The people making the phone calls are the

Grinders in a telemarketing company. The Grinders put the cars together in an automobile manufacturing plant.

Grinders are essential for the growth of any company. It is important for a Finder to understand the key attributes of a Grinder, which are they:

- Work only in the present
- Do not like to delegate
- Distrust Finders and Minders
- Like doing one thing at a time
- Will do as instructed, but will rarely generate new ideas

The Finder usually understands how to do the Grinders work. That is why it is easy for a Finder to hire supervisors and managers to make sure the Grinders are doing a good job. The Finder can usually listen to a phone call or observe a production process to see that the Grinder is doing a good or a bad job. It is usually hard for the Grinder to pull the wool over the eyes of a Finder.

Conversely, Grinders can typically fool Minders. Minders usually do not know how Grinders do their work.

A Different Time Zone

B2B truism: *Grinders are only concerned about what happens today. No concern is given to the past or the future.*

Grinders work in a different time zone than do Finders and Minders. They only care about today. A manufacturing Grinder only cares about the number of widgets to be finished today. A telemarketing Grinder only cares about the number of phone calls to be made today. They give no thought to what has happened in the company during the past. They are not concerned about the future. They assume that someone in management will provide the materials or other resources needed to do their jobs tomorrow. They often do not care about the customer. Their goal is to get through today, go home, have a pizza and go bowling or watch television. There is no worry about tomorrow for the Grinder because they assume the Finders or Minders will provide tomorrow's resources.

Grinders typically have a strong distrust for Finders and Minders. If you call a company meeting the first thing the Grinder will think is, *"What are they going to take away from me today?"* They frequently think that Finders and Minders are working against them by wanting to deny them raises, health benefits, profit-sharing and other such items. They will often bolt from the company if they are offered a little more money from a competitor.

I am not going to spend a lot of time on Grinders in this book because Finders usually understand how Grinders do their work. Finders also usually know how to motivate and train Grinders.

Finders, however, often find it difficult to understand why Grinders distrust them. It is a fact of life; just don't take it personally. Your job as a Finder, as it relates to Grinders, is to deliver your product or service at the lowest possible cost. This may mean that you will not give pay raises in the future. This may mean that you will be forced to cut back on health care or other benefits in order to be competitive. That is your job and that is one of the reasons it is lonely at the top.

CHAPTER 6

Tempting a Good Person

There is too much theft happening with employees today. They steal money, time, inventory, intellectual property and other assets. I am sharing the following stories with you in an attempt to educate you on some of the possible ways people steal.

$1,000,000 Theft

I received a phone call a few years ago from a CEO about two weeks after she discovered that her "trusted controller" had stolen a little over $1,000,000 from the company. She was referred to me by an attorney who thought I might be of assistance in trying to salvage the company. The company was a third-generation manufacturing company that employed about 150 people.

The controller who had stolen the money was gone from the premises when I was hired, so I learned everything about the theft after she had been terminated.

This was a heart-wrenching experience to witness. The CEO had trusted this controller for nearly a decade. The CEO's trust was demonstrated by her giving the controller a lot of responsibilities, but it did *not* include check signing. Additionally, the company had an independent CPA firm issue quarterly unaudited reviewed financial statements (UAR), which gave the owner a certain amount of comfort related to the company's cash and inventory because of the quarterly financial statements issued by the company's independent CPA firm.

Regarding theft insurance, the company previously had a $1,000,000 insurance policy for theft and fraud, but the controller talked the owner and the insurance company into reducing the insurance by 90% a couple of years before the fraud was detected.

The fraud was very simple. The controller wrote checks to herself in amounts of $6,000 to $8,000 a month for several years. The money was used to fund a prescription drug habit. The bank cashed the forged checks and was able, to the shock and dismay of the CEO, to get out of any responsibility for the fraud. The checks were coded to cost of goods sold. There was no "segregation of duties" in the company's internal control system, so the fraud was easy to do and easy to hide from the owner. I believe a lawsuit was filed against the independent CPA firm, but I do not know the resolution of the claim.

The damage to the company from the fraud was too much, and the owner sold the company assets to an out-of-state buyer. Almost all of the 150 or so employees lost their jobs because of the company's lack of internal controls that lead to the theft. A third-generation company was killed, not because of any market constraints or competition, but because the company's controller was able to take money that did not belong to her. A company was forced to sell its assets at a discount and 150 or more families were damaged in the aftermath - tragedy beyond words or description.

$125,000 Theft

Within a few weeks of being hired by a company, we found that the client's finance manager was stealing money. The finance manager had been with the company for some time. We noticed that one particular vendor was listed twice in the company's vendor list. The odd thing about that was the second of the two names of the vendor had a couple of letters transposed. We found that checks had been written to the name of the vendor with the transposed letters. The checks were written in even amounts each week over a long period of time. Upon further examination we discovered these checks were going into the finance manager's personal account. The amount of the theft was about $125,000.

$250,000 Theft

About three weeks after being hired by a retail company, I became weary of the controller not giving me the bank reconciliations. I talked to the owner of the company and was able to obtain copies of bank statements from the company's bank. I had a different staff person help me reconcile the bank statements. We discovered that the controller had a three-person scheme to steal from the company. The controller would write a check to one of the company's vendors and hand-deliver the check to a friend. His friend would take the check to a bank teller who would cash the check. The three people (the controller, the friend and the bank teller) would then split the cash proceeds. The thieves were caught by the work performed by my firm. Some relatives of the dishonest controller personally borrowed money and paid the owner about $250,000. To my knowledge, the crime was never reported to the authorities.

Inventory Theft

After my firm had worked for a retail client
for about a year, I noticed that the inventory
was shrinking in a certain type of merchandise.
We double-checked the numbers and did
physical counts. To our dismay, the merchandise
continued to shrink. We created plans with the
owner of the company to determine what was
causing the inventory shrinkage. We eventually
discovered that a sales person and the dock
manager were stuffing inventory into empty
boxes that would be thrown into the company's
dumpster. The sales person and the dock
manager knew the approximate time the dump
truck would stop by each evening to empty the
dumpster, which was after the retailer closed the
doors. The two company employees would wait
together after the store closed its doors. They
would then back their vehicles to the dumpster,
take the merchandise out of the boxes and
throw the stolen merchandise into their trunks
before the dump truck emptied the dumpster.
The thieves were eventually caught. The
company was able to catch the theft due to the
implementation of internal controls on inventory
shrinkage that my firm recommended.

Credit Card and Check Theft

This was an odd situation, but it shows how creative certain employees can be when it comes to stealing from an employer.

A new accounts payable clerk was given the responsibility to cut checks from a pre-approved list. She was not given the authority to sign the checks. She cut a check to a national credit card company and the check was signed by the owner. The credit card company happened to be the same one the clerk used to purchase gasoline for her own personal use. The clerk sent the company's check to her credit card company, which applied the check to the clerk's credit card account.

The accounts payable clerk became more confident and cut a check to her mother's mortgage company. The check was signed by a hurried business owner who trusted the clerk. The check was sent to the clerk's mother's mortgage company and was cashed. Fortunately, these two items were discovered and the clerk was fired. In both cases, internal control measures were not followed by check signers and a devious accounts payable clerk quickly picked up on steps that were skipped by the owners.

Two Weeks After Being Hired

One of my clients had a very good controller who was very honest and was trusted by all in the company. When she quit for personal reasons the company ran an advertisement in the newspaper to find a new controller. They quickly found a person who was immediately available. (The fact that the new controller could start working the next day should have been a clue that something was wrong.)

This was a retail environment in which some cash sales were made by customers. The new controller opened a personal bank account at the company's bank and started taking the company's bank deposits to the bank instead of delegating this duty to others. (This should have been a second clue for the company that something was wrong.) The controller took cash from the company's deposit and put the money into his personal bank account. This happened within the first two weeks of this controller being hired! Fortunately, my client had good segregation of duties, and the theft was caught immediately. The dishonest controller was fired.

Sometime after firing the dishonest controller the company discovered this person had stolen significant sums of money from his previous employer.

B2B truism: *Far too many white-collar crimes committed by Minders are not reported to the legal authorities, which allows the Minder to steal from future employers.*

Money Owed to the IRS

I was called into a company shortly after the controller took off with IRS money withheld from employee's checks. The controller filed the IRS forms on time and checks were cut by the company to pay the taxes to the IRS. However, the controller did not send the checks to the IRS. Instead, he changed the name on the checks and put the IRS money into his own personal bank account.

To make matters worse, this controller had access to the company's file server. Prior to being caught in the theft he went into the computer room and stole the hard drive from the file server! Unfortunately, the company did not have an off-site backup of the file server.

The IT Department

One of my favorite consultants has a saying that goes something like, *"It's not what they do during the day, but it's what cockroaches do at night, when you can't see what they are doing, that causes all the problems."*

Now, I'm *not* comparing your IT department to cockroaches, but the analogy fits.

Can you say that you know what your IT people are doing with your money? Can you say, for a certainty, that your money is being spent wisely on the correct technology? Do you know for a fact that customer lists and other intellectual property are safeguarded?

Typically, the company's IT person does the following:

(1) Requests the action
(2) Approves the action
(3) Executes the action

"When the same person can request the action, approve the action and then execute it, all of the ingredients are in place for problems.

"Businesses face a particularly vexing challenge in preventing fraud by IT 'superusers' such as network administrators and senior managers. These individuals may be able to create 'ghost' employees, fake vendor accounts or fraudulent purchase orders and invoices."[12]

Please do not hear what I am *not* saying: Nobody can guarantee an owner against theft. We can, however, talk about such items as "internal control systems," and "segregation of duties." These terms may seem vague to a Finder, but they are tangible and necessary. Finders, keep in mind that I am not suggesting that you need to live in fear that you can't trust your key employees.

Business owners, without realizing it, often put employees in a situation where the temptation to steal is simply too great for them to resist. Ultimately, it is the business owner's fault for putting the employee in a situation that allowed the employee to steal.

B2B truism: *We often find that many business owners unintentionally place their employees in a position to steal from the company.*

A news article supports this theory that people steal because they simply are allowed to do so by the owners of companies:

> "The number of local cases involving employee theft are on the rise. In a matter of months, several investigations have been conducted, including two that led to recent convictions."

> "Hibbing Deputy Chief Duane Gielen and investigator Dale Wright have felt the increase in such cases. The pair have uncovered theft of more than $128,000 in four recent cases. 'The no. 1 reason they take is because they can,' said Gielen. 'The opportunity is there and they take it.'"[13]

The Problem of Employee Theft

Another interesting article "The Problem of Employee Theft," reads:

> "Although it's not a pleasant topic to discuss, the fact is that theft by employees of small businesses totals nearly $40 billion in this country each year.

"As hard as it is to believe that someone you hire to fill a trusted position in your company would actually take from you, it happens every day in all kinds of businesses and in a variety of ways. And it is estimated that up to 75 percent of all employee theft goes unnoticed.

"Some security experts predict that up to 30 percent of the nation's workers will steal at some time in their career. Difficult economic times, lack of salary increases and the threats of downsizing and cutbacks make it even more tempting for employees to help themselves.

"Employee theft can take many forms, from stealing office supplies or merchandise, to stealing time by improperly reporting sick leave and vacation to stealing intellectual property and confidential information. When employee theft is discovered, the employer/owner feels violated and often reacts out of emotion."

"If you are the victim of employee theft, the first thing you should do is take a thorough look at your company processes. Theft usually occurs as a result of a breakdown in procedure. Do you lack a system for checks and balances? Are employees not following clearly defined procedures? Are you paying enough attention? Use the situation as a wake-up call to re-examine the way you do business.

"Don't assume that well-paid employees will resist the temptation to steal, or that trusted employees will report others who steal. Don't assume that new employees are more likely to steal than those with the most seniority. Remember that things change in our employees' lives just like they do in ours. Increased debt load from a child in college, strained personal relationships, an addiction or pressure from peers could all change a long-time, trusted employee's attitude.

"Remove the opportunity to steal. Establish a system of checks and balances and oversight for key processes that ensures different people are performing tasks and can routinely check one another's work. Have an outside auditor perform an unscheduled inspection from time to time. Ensure that employees responsible for accounting and financial functions take time off routinely so irregularities in their work are more easily spotted.

"Realize that theft often occurs when employees are under personal financial stress.

"Finally, be a positive role model. The tone for integrity and trust starts at the top of any organization. Talk the talk and walk the walk. Set an example of ethical behavior and equitable management." [14]

Regarding the last paragraph, one of my clients caught an employee that was cheating on her time card and was being paid for time not worked. The client asked me to terminate the employee. I agreed to perform the task. I vividly remember the conversation. I asked, "*Susie (not her real name), tell me why you cheated on your time card. Was stealing this small amount of money really worth it to you?*" Her response caught me off guard. She replied that she stole the money because she saw the owner pocket cash from the cash register.

Obviously, the fact that the owner takes money from the company is no excuse for an employee doing the same but the last paragraph of the above article bears repeating:

"The tone for integrity and trust starts at the top of any organization. Talk the talk and walk the walk. Set an example of ethical behavior and equitable management."

Don't give your employees an excuse to be dishonest or unethical because they perceive you act that way. Be above reproach with the cash and assets of your company.

Steal From My Own Company?

I have witnessed numerous Finders put the company's cash into their pockets. I'm not sure why they do this, but I imagine they say something like the following to themselves, *"This is my company and my money, and I will use it as I see fit."*

Well, the above statement may be true to the business owner; however, Finders who pocket cash (without proper documentation) will find themselves in a situation where the adage comes true: *Perception becomes reality.*

The perceptions by company employees when an owner pockets cash become reality to them. I have heard statements from employees such as the following regarding this subject:

- The owner is trying to cheat his partner, partners or spouse.

- The owner is trying to cheat the IRS by taking the cash and not paying taxes. Perhaps the company will get into trouble if the owner cheats the IRS.

- The owner has told us numerous times that the company can't afford to make pay raises, yet look at how much cash he is taking from the company.

As Finders, we do not want a negative perception to become a reality. We want to set the right example and be the leaders that people can look up to and respect at all times.

Fraud Insurance

A company should always have good theft and fraud insurance. This is one area that should be reviewed and possibly increased at the annual renewal of the insurance each year.

The next chapter explains some of the proactive things a Finder might consider to stop employee theft.

CHAPTER 7

Who is Watching your Controller?

Much of the theft that we see is done by the company's Minders, usually the controller or accounting manager. (These people are sometimes called bookkeepers, finance managers, etc.)

There is a second serious problem with Minders regarding theft from other company employees. Minders are usually not trained to catch fraud perpetrated by other company employees. They simply do not have the experience, expertise, training or skills to detect sophisticated fraud committed by other employees.

Who is watching your controller?

Did you notice the advice about this subject in the previous chapter, in the article, *The Problem with Employee Theft*"? The middle of the seventh paragraph reads:

"Have an outside auditor perform an unscheduled inspection from time to time."

Do you have an outside professional coming into your place of business each month (perhaps unannounced) to look over the accounting records, computer systems, walk around the plant and observe the trends on the financial statements or systems? If not, perhaps you should consider hiring such a person or firm.

My CPA Firm?

Many business owners ask B2B if their CPA or CPA firm can perform the function of looking over the shoulders of the controller and staff. This is a good and legitimate question.

Certain, but not all, CPA firms can be hired to perform fraud examinations. This is a specific engagement that will last for the limited period of time that the CPA firm is engaged.

CPA firms are usually engaged to perform tax returns, audits, unaudited reviews and/or compilations. *They should not be relied upon for fraud detection when they perform any of these engagements, unless the engagement letter specifically spells out the terms of the fraud detection.*

It is not fair to the business owner or the CPA firm to expect fraud detection unless the scope of work is so defined in the CPAs engagement letter. Read the engagement letter from your CPA very carefully. Most audit, compilation and unaudited review engagement letters will say something like, *"Our engagement cannot be relied upon to disclose errors, illegal acts, fraud or any theft that may exist in your company."*

Again, there is nothing wrong with your CPA making this type of statement; you just need to be aware that the scope of the CPAs work will most likely not uncover any fraud or theft that may exist in your company.

B2B truism: *Do not rely upon your CPA firm to detect theft or fraud, unless you specifically engage them for this function.*

Most CPA firms need to keep some distance from creating the internal controls of their clients. This is called "independence" and is an important function of our society. Otherwise, they might be viewed by the public as "auditing themselves."

Arthur Andersen's trouble with Enron is an example. Apparently, Arthur Andersen was paid more money to perform "consulting" services than it was being paid for "audit" services. The *perception* in the business community was that

Andersen's auditors were closing their eyes to certain types of questionable business activities that should have been made known to the business community and stockholders.

Arthur Andersen & Co. has been vindicated in the courts on this matter, but the *perception* led to the company's death.

From January 15th to April 15th

The key partners of CPA firms are usually not available to the business owner between January 15th and April 15th. The partners of CPA firms have intentionally created a business model that causes them to be too busy to leave their offices to spend quality time with a client during the busy season. This statement also holds true for most of the non-busy season.

To compensate for the lack of partner time, these firms sometimes send out inexperienced staff people to perform consulting services. By "inexperienced," I mean they do not have a lot of tenure working *within* a closely-held company and are not senior-level executives with 20-plus years of experience.

Fraud and Experience

It is risky to assume that professionals, just because they have a CPA certificate, are experienced enough to catch fraud. Most CPA firms that do income tax preparation and audit work have spent their entire careers in an accounting firm. They typically have not worked full-time as a CFO or controller. As such, they may or may not have the experience to detect sophisticated fraud in your company.

Basic accounting (debits and credits) is a very small part of fraud detection. An accounting degree and a license do not always mean a CPA or the firm's staff is qualified to understand the complexities of someone trying to steal from your company. One must have years of training and experience for fraud detection.

Senior-level Executives

As a business owner, you need a seasoned senior-level executive to watch over the shoulders of your controller.

We recommend that you engage this person to come into your place of business *at least once a month*. Allow him or her to look into the computer system and look at the details of the financial statements. Let him or her walk around the building or the plant to see what is happening with the company.

Meet regularly with this person to receive input as to what is happening with your business. Let your accounting and IT staff be trained by this person. Let your accounting and other staff know that a seasoned professional is looking over their shoulders. This should help reduce your staff's temptation to steal.

Additionally, this senior-level executive should be expected to help the company develop internal control systems and segregation of duties.

A Second Opinion By Your CPA

After doing the above, have your CPA firm take another look at the financial statements for the company in an independent function. Create a situation where your CPA firm and your senior-level executives are on your team to advise you and give you input from a variety of different perspectives. This teamwork between the two different levels of disciplines should help you with your goals to decrease employee theft.

No professional can or should promise a complete elimination of fraud. There are ways, however, to prepare a strategy to help reduce or minimize fraud in your company.

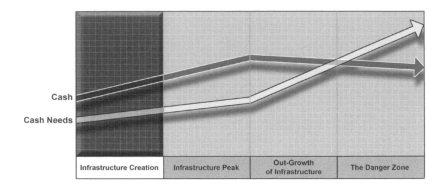

| Infrastructure Creation | Infrastructure Peak | Out-Growth of Infrastructure | The Danger Zone |

Cash

Cash Needs

CHAPTER 8

Infrastructure Creation

You have been creating your company's infrastructure since the day you started your business. Admittedly, you may not have been doing this intentionally, but you have made the effort, regardless of your intentions.

What Is Infrastructure?

The word infrastructure is relatively new to our business vocabulary. The history and business definitions are:

"An underlying base or foundation especially for an organization or system.

"The term *infrastructure* has been used since 1927 to refer collectively to the roads, bridges, rail lines, and similar public works that are required for an industrial economy, or a portion of it, to function.

"Perhaps because of the word's technical sound, people now use *infrastructure* to refer to any substructure or underlying system."[15]

Your Business Infrastructure

Most Finders do not methodically create a plan to build the infrastructure of the company. Rather, they typically take a Band Aid approach and create the infrastructure from necessity and not from long-term planning. We will spend more time on this in later chapters, but a short list of the Finder's infrastructure might include some of the following:

- Employees
- Vendors
- Computer hardware
- Computer software
- Outside contractors
- Bankers
- Lenders or leasing companies
- Outside accountants and attorneys
- Operating procedures and processes

- IT staff
- Machinery and equipment
- Office space or buildings
- Websites
- Voice telephone systems
- Etc.

In the beginning, the infrastructures (systems) that Finders create are usually oriented around customer activities. The activities typically involve:

- Finding customers
- Closing the sale
- Delivering the goods or services
- Invoicing
- Collecting cash

I sometimes refer to this period as the "dating" period. Life is good. The Finder is totally focused on the customer. Tremendous efforts are made to find the customer, listen to his needs, solve his problems and deliver the goods or services before the due date.

B2B truism: *Most Finders do not spend a lot of time methodically planning their business infrastructure.*

Short Cash Cycles

The cash cycle is typically short in this period. It is easy to get the invoice to the proper people and to have a quick turn-around on the money for the invoice. Overhead is typically low in the company and, while cash is tight, the Finder has a gut feeling that "this will work" and that there will always be more cash than expenses. The little bit of excess cash allows the Finder to invest in more infrastructure. The Finder invests in people, machines, equipment and other things that will allow the company to have even greater sales than before.

Time With the Customer

The Finder spends time with the customer and develops a relationship with the customer's key people. The Finder has a lot of energy in this period and spends much "creative time" in meeting the needs of the customer in a manner that sets the Finder apart from the competition. There are few administrative distractions during this period that might take the Finder away from the focus of the customer.

Information System Infrastructure

"A well-designed information system rests on a coherent foundation that supports modifications as new business or administrative initiatives arise. Known as the information system infrastructure, the foundation consists of core telecommunications networks, databases, software, hardware, and procedures. Managed by various specialists, information systems frequently incorporate the use of general information and telecommunication utilities, such as the Internet. Owing to business globalization, an organization's infrastructure often crosses many national boundaries. Creating and maintaining such a complex infrastructure requires extensive planning and consistent implementation to handle strategic corporate initiatives."[16]

The infrastructure changes and impacts everyone who is involved with your company as your company continues to grow.

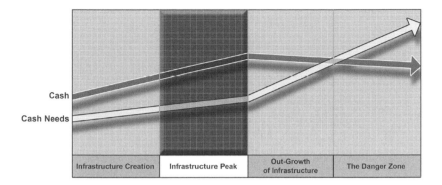

Cash			
Cash Needs			
Infrastructure Creation	Infrastructure Peak	Out-Growth of Infrastructure	The Danger Zone

CHAPTER 9

Infrastructure Peak

The Honeymoon Phase

If you take a close look at the graph above, you will see an unusually high gap between the company's cash and cash needs. I call this the honeymoon period, or "Infrastructure Peak."

Another economic term for this period might be the ROI (return on investment). This period is the effect of a significant focus by the Finder during Infrastructure Creation. This period is an aberration, in a business sense, and typically gives the Finder a false sense of security about the future of the company.

For every cause, there is an effect. The *cause* of Infrastructure Creation leads to the *effect* of Infrastructure Peak.

The reason I refer to this cycle as the "honeymoon" period is because it gives a false sense of security about the company. The company has not yet experienced the "morning after." There has been such a focus on the vision of the company and the customer that an economic aberration has occurred. The aberration involves the following:

- High customer service
- Short cash collection cycles
- Few customer complaints
- Low overhead
- Personal financial sacrifice by the Finder

Running Lean and Mean

In other words, the company has been running lean, *perhaps too lean*. The Finder and the rest of the company employees have been running a 100-yard dash for about 100 miles. The excess cash gives pause to the Finder and the company employees and begins a thought process that might sound something like:

"Perhaps I should have a pay raise."

"We need more people so we can take time off."

"I bet our customers would like to see us in a better building."

"Don't we need to give out 401(k) and health plans?"

"Let's hire staff to do filing and to answer the phones."

"My spouse wants me to build a new house."

"I really *need* a newer vehicle."

"Can we all go on a vacation to Hawaii?"

"We need more equipment to make better products."

"Should we diversify and find other lines of business?"

Well, you get the idea. I could add many more, but the above sentiments are adequate to show the change in attitude. "Lean and mean" is no longer the mantra of the company. *Less thought is given to the needs of the customer during this period of time.*

More thought and energy is devoted to building "the company." The Finder starts to get pulled into directions that are unfamiliar by a host of professionals and other people who seemingly know more than the business owner about how to use the company's cash. Plans and methods are created to have cash leave the company.

More resources are spent in buying things that do not always lead to excellent customer service.

Customers Who Get In the way?

I remember a conversation I overheard while I was at a client's office in the mid 1980s. The executives of the company were lamenting that the customers were getting in the way.

I remember hearing one of the most foolish comments I have heard in my career when one executive exclaimed that he could get much more done if the customer would simply *"not get in the way."* I stared with incredulity at this seemingly intelligent person. It was not the right time to express my feelings, but I wanted to shout, *"Don't you understand that the customer is the one paying your paycheck?"* This was unbelievable, but is not uncommon for certain people who lose track of trying to fill the needs of the customer.

Infrastructure Outgrowth described in the next chapter is the *effect* of some of the *causes* that start to occur in the Infrastructure Peak.

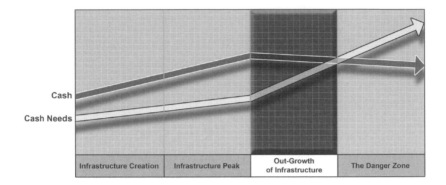

Cash
Cash Needs

| Infrastructure Creation | Infrastructure Peak | Out-Growth of Infrastructure | The Danger Zone |

CHAPTER 10

Outgrowth of Infrastructure

The Foundation Has Cracked

Let's imagine that you have built a building in which your company operates. The building has a good foundation. Because of land limitations, the only way you can expand your building is by adding additional floors. The sales of your company are growing rapidly. You need more space so you decide to add an additional floor to the existing building.

The expansion is a success until the sales of your company take another leap. You need more space and decide to add yet another floor to the building. Before the new floor is completed your contractor notifies you that the foundation has started to crack. You are advised to stop the construction. Not only have you wasted money on the new floor but you now are concerned that you might not be able to take care of the increased customer sales that are presently on the books.

The above is analogous to most growth companies. From the first day of opening the company, the Finder is building a foundation, which we call "infrastructure." As we discussed earlier in this book, this foundation, or infrastructure, is made of the company's employees, vendors, computer hardware and software, bankers, lenders, outside professionals, operating procedures, IT staff, office space, buildings, equipment, websites, telephone systems and so forth.

Infrastructure Outgrowth

Companies that experience significant growth, both in sales and the volume of transactions, typically outgrow their infrastructure.

The business reason for the outgrowth is simple: The Finder has been so busy bringing in sales that attention has not been given to the foundation (infrastructure) of the company.

The volume of sales, transactions, employees, etc., has a collective "weight." The company's infrastructure foundation has major "cracks" and cannot support the stress of the weight. Thus, the company experiences infrastructure outgrowth. The company must now stop its normal process of sales and delivery to strengthen the foundation; otherwise, the entire company is in jeopardy.

Symptoms of the Infrastructure Outgrowth

Before we discuss the causes of this problem, let's discuss some of the *symptoms* of the problem. The symptoms of infrastructure outgrowth are easy to spot and typically are demonstrated by some of the following:

Customers

- Customer complaints increase
- Customers begin disputing charges on invoices or statements
- Customer refusal to accept certain goods or services
- Orders from certain customers unexpectedly decrease
- More time is spent on the problems with smaller customers than with larger or more profitable customers

Productivity

- Quality of goods or service decreases
- Accounting starts giving out inaccurate information
- The Finder needs to attend more meetings
- Finders and Minders have longer "non-productive" work weeks
- Equipment down-time that is higher than normal
- Information from accounting is delayed

Employees

- Overtime increases
- Workforce turnover is higher
- Employee theft of money, time, inventory, and customer lists increases
- Employee benefit costs, such as COBRA, training, etc., increases
- Quality of new hires of employees decreases
- Department of Labor audits increase

Cash & Company Assets

- Average days a receivable is collectable increases
- There are periodic shortages of cash
- Inventory that is not sellable increases

- The owner or owners start lending money to the company to cover overhead

Software, Websites, Computer Hardware

- Computer crashes occur more frequently
- Viruses or other software problems arise
- The telephone or voice mail systems become inadequate or very expensive to operate
- IT unexpectedly and constantly requests computer hardware purchases
- Website problems take longer to fix
- Bids to convert to new software products are higher than expected
- The owner feels there is a never-ending black hole of money spent on computers and systems, with no end in sight

Vendors

- Vendors start delaying delivery to your company
- Vendors are not paid on time and become disillusioned
- Valuable time is spent finding new vendors

Overhead

- Overhead expenses increase unexpectedly
- Legal and professional fees increase

- Insurance costs increase significantly
- Company receives fines & notices from the IRS or other governmental agencies
- Health insurance rates significantly increase
- The number of FMV leases increases

Lending & Borrowing

- The costs of borrowing money increase
- Company is not able to borrow enough money from banks or lenders
- Company receives unexpected requests for documents from banks or lenders
- Banker complaints about the accuracy of internal accounting documents increase
- Banker complaints about the delay of accounting information increase
- The Finder perceives that bankers or lenders are backing away from the company

This list could be much longer but you get the idea. The company is not running on all cylinders and the problems seem to compound daily.

The Problem

One of the most valuable educations that I have experienced in my career was working for

Arthur Andersen & Co. As I stated earlier in this book, I left the company in 1985 as a manager. The high quality of people and the standards that were present in those days were second to none. The managing partner in Phoenix and many of my colleagues were an inspiration. I credit AA & Co. for much of the success in my career. The problems the firm experienced many years after I left have not diminished my respect and admiration for working for the best the world had to offer at that time.

When I became a manager with the firm, I noticed a trend with the engagements that went well and those that did not. Without exception, the engagements that went well (under budget, satisfied clients who paid their fees, contented partners, etc) included a high amount of planning before the work began.

Conversely, the projects that did not go well had a common denominator: Someone cut corners and did not put in the time to adequately plan for success. Looking back, I am not sure why corners were cut on the planning phase. Perhaps we were too busy or were concerned about trying to get as many billable hours as possible. I'm not sure of the reasons, but I am convinced of the results.

I quickly found that the planning phase of any project took a lot of discipline. It also took time to make inquiries of people who were more knowledgeable than me on certain topics. I learned to swallow my pride and ask the questions in order to create success. Some of the planning took research. I vividly remember reading books late into the evenings trying to gain knowledge about certain topics. I also had to incur time (money) that perhaps was not viewed as productive before the project even began.

In the above paragraph, I identified some of the items needed for adequate planning:

- Time
- Discipline
- Research
- Money

B2B truism: *Long-term planning takes time, money and discipline from the Finder.*

Now let's discuss the problem that creates the "symptoms" which are described earlier in this chapter. This may not be fun reading for you; however, you need to grind through this in order to avoid the negative symptoms caused by the problem.

Planning for a Growth Company

Finders, by definition, are visionaries, dreamers, idea generators, innovators, motivators and catalysts for change. Do you notice something missing from this list? How about the word "planners"?

Finders, by definition, loathe detailed planning of infrastructure. It is boring to them. They do not like the tedious work. They typically are not skilled in the subjects related to the infrastructure of their company. Finders get frustrated spending time listening to "geeks" or other professionals who not only cost a lot of money but seem to be self-serving. They do not see the benefit of spending hours, days, weeks or months in detailed planning of infrastructure. To a Finder, this planning time takes away from finding customers and building the company.

B2B truism: *The failure to plan infrastructure will eventually hurt the company and will take away time from finding customers at some point in the future.*

Planning Comments from Others

Some successful people have commented on the importance of planning, from which we can all learn:

"In the absence of clearly defined goals, we are forced to concentrate on activity and ultimately become enslaved by it."[17]

"To succeed in anything it is necessary to know the rules and understand how to apply them. It is necessary to study, to learn, to think, and to plan."[18]

Work Your Weakness

As a Finder, there is nothing wrong with admitting that you do not like detailed planning of infrastructure. If you do not like it, do not do it. It is your responsibility, however, to make sure it gets done.

The Future of Your Company

Let me help you get started on this process. I'd like you fill in the blanks next to the following questions:

Estimate your gross company sales:

This year: $ _____

Five years from now: $ _____

Ten years from now: $ _____

Name your three most dangerous competitors:

1. _____

2. _____

3. _____

Now you are ready to answer three key
questions. The answers to these questions
may take some time for you to complete. Be as
detailed as you can and write down the answers
to these questions.

1. What are your most dangerous competitors
   planning to do to take away your customers?

2. What do you need to do to keep ahead of your
   most dangerous competitors who will be
   actively trying to keep you from achieving
   your sales goal ten years from now?

3. Who is going to be on your team to build your infrastructure to help achieve the level of sales you want ten years from now and to help keep your company from being killed by your most dangerous competition?

Share This Information

Share the above information with your team. If you do not have the right team players, go get them. It is better to get them on board with your company than to possibly have them hired by your competitors.

Share the sales goals that you want to achieve five and ten years from now, plus the other information you documented from this exercise.

Assign your team to arrive at a budget to build the infrastructure needed to support your goals.

The Job as a Finder

In short, your job as a Finder is as follows:

1. Set the sales goal for five and ten years from now.

2. Hire the right people to build the company's infrastructure.

3. Give the right people the money to achieve your infrastructure.

4. Make sure your infrastructure team does as assigned. Fire them if they fail and replace them with better people.

5. Go find customers, open new markets, dream and have some fun.

B2B truism: *Your competitors are actively planning today to take away your customers tomorrow.*

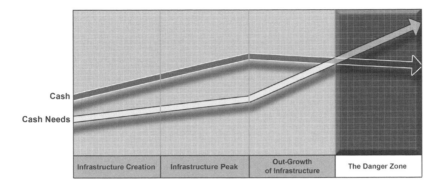

| Infrastructure Creation | Infrastructure Peak | Out-Growth of Infrastructure | The Danger Zone |

CHAPTER 11

The Danger Zone

If you look at the graph above you will notice that the cash needs of the company exceed the available cash. This is *The Danger Zone*. Bluntly put, the future of the company is in jeopardy.

There are dozens of reasons why the cash needs exceed the available cash. I outlined some of those reasons in the preceding chapters, which deal with the outgrowth of the company's infrastructure.

Regardless of the reasons, the company is either in serious trouble or is headed that way.

B2B truism: *The Danger Zone is created when the cash needs of your company far exceed the cash available to meet those needs.*

Another Analogy

Let's imagine you have a friend or a relative who is severely overweight. This person's doctor has made it clear that the weight must decrease or severe consequences will follow. This person tells you that he or she has a plan to decrease the weight. The self-created plan from your friend is to increase the daily calories that are to be consumed. Your response might be, *"How can you lose weight by increasing the number of calories you have been consuming in the past?"* There is no response to your question.

The above is analogous to what happens to Finders when they hit The Danger Zone. They then begin to *increase* the activities that *cause harm* to the company. Why do Finders get involved in this phenomenon? Well, this chapter explores the answer to this question.

Controlling the "Finding" Time

The inception of a company is somewhat of a romantic time for Finders. Yes, there are cash flow and other business problems, but the enjoyment the Finder has in the finding activities seems to outweigh other issues. Sometimes, for the first time in their lives, the Finders are actually getting to do what they want to do for a living. Some are golfing with key people; some are thinking and dreaming; some are spending time with intelligent associates working on the details of *the dream*.

Before the business honeymoon is over, the romantic finding activities give an euphoric sense of fulfillment and joy to the Finders. They can put up with pain from others as long as they can spend the majority of their time in finding activities. The future looks bright to the Finder, even if there is little or no cash in the company.

The business honeymoon is over when the Finder stops spending most of his or her time in finding activities. Seemingly overnight, the Finder is spending most of his or her time doing administrative and other non-finding activities.

B2B truism: *We have yet to see a Finder start a business so he can spend his time on accounting and computer problems, yet far too many spend too much time doing those things.*

What went wrong after the business honeymoon? Well, the weight of the infrastructure has caused the Finder's time to shift to non-finding activities.

Figuratively speaking, instead of spending time on things that used to be fun, the Finder is now spending each day of the week cleaning out the garage and raking the leaves in the yard.

The Finder's Time Shift

So, the trend slowly moves from being a Finder toward becoming a Minder.

The Finder's time shift is predictable during these transitional phases. The following information should not be viewed in terms of absolutes but as observations of trends, based upon decades of experience watching Finders become Minders during The Danger Zone:

Activity	Infra-structure Growth	Infra-structure Peak	Out-Growth of Infra-structure	The Danger Zone
Finding	85%	80%	70%	30%
Minding	5%	15%	25%	60%
Grinding	10%	5%	5%	10%
	100%	100%	100%	100%

A graph of the shift to minding time would look something like the following:

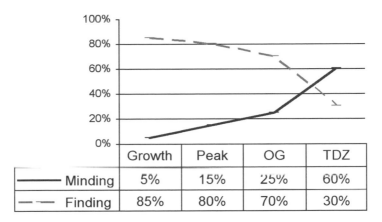

	Growth	Peak	OG	TDZ
——— Minding	5%	15%	25%	60%
– – Finding	85%	80%	70%	30%

Activities During the Time Shift

You will recall that in Chapter 9 we discussed that a Finder's principle goal is to build relationships that cause the company to grow. We identified a few things that Finders do during the Infrastructure Creation period of the company, such as:

- Building relationships with customers
- Creating relationships with vendors
- Delegating tasks to employees or associates
- Causing sales and cash to come into the company

During the time shift from finding to minding we see the Finder do less and less of the above.

Instead of finding, the Finder starts minding activities such as:

- Creating cash-flow statements
- Meeting at length with accounting and administrative staff
- Many meetings with bankers and lenders
- Meetings with attorneys and accountants
- Spending significant time deciding which checks will be written
- Purchasing and hooking up computers
- Installing computer software
- Entering transactions into the computer
- Firing of staff
- Hiring of new staff (who typically are not trained properly)
- Taking deposits to the bank
- Writing checks

A person might ask, *"What is wrong with these activities?"* Good question, which is easily answered:

- Finders are not good at doing most, if any of the above. They do not have the skills, patience or time to properly train or to perform these tasks.

- All of the above take the Finder away from finding activities, which often has serious consequences.

Consequences of the Time Shift

During The Danger Zone, the Finder is dealing with infrastructure "weight" that distracts and then eventually destroys. The destruction may be in several forms, such as:

- Death of the company
- Loss of current customers
- Damaged business relationships due to stress to the Finder
- Death of the dream of the Finder
- Loss of enthusiasm or energy by the Finder
- Divorce
- Damaged relationships with children and family members
- Diminished health of the Finder
- Loss of future customers

The destruction items above do not include the damage to employees, families of employees, vendors and other relationships of the Finder.

Why Does a Finder Become a Minder?

Why do you think that Finders stop doing what they love to do, which are finding activities, and start doing what they hate to do, which are minding activities?

The answer to the question is very simple; however, the discipline needed to find the solution to the problem may be complex. Most likely, the Finder will need outside help during The Danger Zone.

I Will Fix the Problem

Most Finders are A+ personalities. Many were in athletics when they were younger and are very competitive. Most have helped the company grow from the sheer efforts of their personalities and skills. Problems, some of them of a serious nature, have arisen in the past. When those problems arose, the Finder jumped in with both feet and solved the problem. Presto! Job completed!

The Changes Are Not So Easy This Time

The infrastructure problems of the company are not so easily fixed today. There is too much weight from infrastructure problems with customers, vendors, employees, subcontractors, computers, bankers, governmental agencies, cash shortages and so forth. More knowledge on how to fix the infrastructure is needed than presently exists within the company.

Someone to Trust

Finders often do not delegate certain tasks to people simply because they do not trust others within the company. In this situation, we need to ask two questions:

1. Is the problem with the Finder?
2. Is the problem with the Minder or Grinder?

The solution to the dilemma may be a difficult one to find if the Finder is the reason for the lack of trust. Sometimes the lack of trust is because the company does not have written policies and procedures (infrastructure) that give comfort to the Finder that the job will be done correctly. Often, the Finder feels that nobody can do the job correctly. *Sometimes the Finder simply has an issue with trust.* If this is the case, it may be good for the Finder to find a confidant to whom he can talk about this trust issue. Ultimately, the Finder *must* delegate tasks to people in order to grow the company and to escape The Danger Zone.

B2B truism: *The Finder must learn to trust people. Employees should be terminated from the company if they are not trustworthy.*

Sometimes the trust issue is because of the prior actions of the Minder or Grinder. If the lack of trust is because the Minder or Grinder has stolen or cheated the company, the next action step is very simple to identify: Fire them – even if they are family members. The Finder wants such a person working elsewhere, hopefully for the competition. It is a rare situation in which the Finder will be able to rehabilitate dishonest employees. If the Finder has dishonest employees, even family members, the Finder has only one course of action, and that is to terminate the relationship and hire someone who is trustworthy.

B2B truism: *Good management is the accomplishment of the goals and objectives of the company through the actions of other people.*

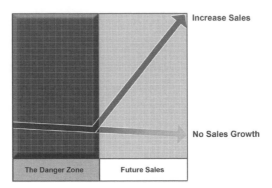

CHAPTER 12

Escaping The Danger Zone

Ideally owners of closely held businesses will read this book and apply its principles before their company arrives in The Danger Zone (TDZ). I realize, however, that some business owners may be in this condition before they pick up this book. We need to now address how to get out of The Danger Zone.

Future Sales With the Right Margins

One of two things will happen with a company that enters TDZ: Sales will increase or decrease. *Sales will not stay flat.*

A Finder who will leave minding enough to increase sales (with good profit margins) might have some likelihood of escaping TDZ.

Cash or Sales?

Which came first: The chicken or the egg? Which comes first in the TDZ: Sales or cash? The answer to this question for the Finder is obvious. The Finder will need to find sales and other people will need to find cash. This is where the discussion in earlier chapters of this book about surrounding yourself with senior-level executives is very important.

B2B truism: *During TDZ, the Finder finds sales and the senior-level executives of the company find cash.*

The Danger Zone Results

The options for a company that enters TDZ are limited. A few of the options are:

(1) The Finder changes habits and grows sales, which might result in an escape from TDZ.

(2) Borrow money from friends or relatives.

(3) Sell valuable company or personal assets to put cash into the company.

(4) The Finder escalates the minding activities, which causes sales to decrease, which has the likelihood of a bad exit strategy for the company.

B2B truism: *Leaders make tough decisions. There is no benefit in shuffling chairs on the deck of the Titanic. Leaders look to the future and avoid the icebergs that are in the path of their company.*

The Shift from Minding to Finding

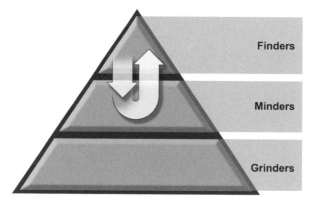

Ultimately, the Finder must leave minding to others to escape The Danger Zone. This shift will take discipline and, possibly some money. There is no choice in the matter. The Finder must find someone who can watch over the minding activities of the company.

CHAPTER 13

Moore's Law and the Finder

Certain laws impact our daily lives, whether or not we are consciously aware of them. For example, the law of gravity is very real. One could argue that it does not exist, but he will change his mind the next time something hard drops on his head.

Let's discuss Moore's Law, an important law that exists with your computer systems. This law is very real. One could argue that it does not exist and is not applicable to one's business. Just like arguing against the law of gravity, however, one will feel a lot of pain with the violation of this law.

Moore's Law Defined

"In 1965, Intel co-founder Gordon Moore saw the future. His prediction, popularly known as Moore's Law, states that the number of transistors on a chip doubles about every two years."[19]

"The observation made in 1965 by Gordon Moore, co-founder of Intel, that the number of transistors per square inch on integrated circuits had doubled every year since the integrated circuit was invented. Moore predicted that this trend would continue for the foreseeable future. In subsequent years, the pace slowed down a bit, but data density has doubled approximately every 18 months, and this is the current definition of Moore's Law, which Moore himself has blessed. Most experts, including Moore himself, expect Moore's Law to hold for at least another two decades."[20]

The Finder may ask, "What does Moore's Law have to do with me?" This is another great question that can be easily answered.

Another Analogy

Suppose you own a growth company and are tired of leasing space from a landlord. You have enough money for the down payment and find a good lender for the balance of the money. You find a good piece of land and make the purchase. You then hire an architect to draw the plans. You go to the city and get the proper zoning. You love the design of the building and can't wait to start construction.

One day you have a meeting with your key staff and show them the building plans. The staff is excited about the project. You show each of them where their new office will be located in the new building. Discussions are made about the office furniture and the decor the new building will have.

One of your employees is very quiet during the entire discussion and does not show any enthusiasm for the project. You notice this person's attitude and ask what is wrong. The employee is reluctant to make a comment and looks embarrassed to speak up in front of all the enthusiastic co-workers. You encourage the employee to speak his mind. With some hesitation he says, *"I hate to say this, but we have been growing in annual sales by about 10 to 15 percent each year for the past several years. Our sales manager is predicting we will keep this sales increase for at least another four years."*

The room grows silent because nobody else understands what this has to do with the design of the new building. *"Are you nuts? What does that have to do with these plans?"* asks one of the co-workers. *"Well,"* the reluctant employee says, *"The way I see things, the size of the building will only accommodate our existing employees. We will outgrow the building before it is even completed. I don't understand why we are constructing a new building that will be too small for our company."*

Dead silence ensues for a minute or so. Then, renewed attention is directed to the plans, which are now scattered all over the office. Measurements are double-checked. Discussions are held about making rooms smaller or making other changes to the building. Ultimately, everyone in the room agrees with our keenly observant employee: The building will be too small for the future growth of the company.

Question: Should the company
(1) construct the building as designed or
(2) change the plans to allow the company to grow?

Answer: Change the plans to allow the company to grow.

Your Company's Computer Infrastructure

The above illustration is applicable to most Finders as it relates to Moore's Law and the company's future growth.

Moore's Law implies that the speed of the "microchips" in your company's computers will double every 18 months. This means that in about 4.5 years from today the speed of future computers will be *three times faster* than the new computer you purchase today. Software designers know this fact and are designing software to accommodate the faster computers that will soon be available.

B2B truism: *Computers 4.5 years from now will be three times faster than computers you purchase today, which means you must have an active computer replacement plan.*

"Why should I be concerned about computers being faster in the future?" a Finder may ask. Another good question, which I can answer.

- Your competitors are making plans to have better technology than your company in order to take away your customers.

- To survive, you need to start budgeting money to replace your existing computer system (file servers, PCs, laptops, modems, routers…the works) at least every two years. Otherwise, you will be behind before you know what hit you.

Computer Planning

Go back to Chapter 11 and look at the sales goals you have for the next ten years. Now, consider filling in the following:

Hardware budget for the next five years:

- Year #1: $_____
- Year #2: $_____
- Year #3: $_____
- Year #4: $_____
- Year #5: $_____

Website, software, intranet and technology budget for the next five years:

- Year #1: $_____
- Year #2: $_____
- Year #3: $_____
- Year #4: $_____
- Year #5: $_____

A Different Level of Thinking

Planning for the future will most likely take a different level of thinking than has been used in the past. Albert Einstein is credited with saying:

"The significant problems we face cannot be solved at the same level of thinking we were at when we created them."[21]

Einstein also said:

"Any intelligent fool can make things bigger and more complex…It takes a touch of genius – and a lot of courage to move in the opposite direction."[22]

And so it goes with the Finder. The Finder cannot expect to be competitive with the company's most dangerous competition unless a new level of thinking is instilled about the future technology of the company. *An identification of money to be spent on future technology must be documented and communicated to key employees, bankers, and trusted advisors.*

This new way of thinking about spending on technology is difficult for some Finders. Some do not trust this way of thinking and feel money would be better spent on other things. Let me give you some advice if you feel this way and are having a difficult time with this topic: Write down the amount of money you feel your *most dangerous competitors* are going to spend on technology in the future. Now, exceed that amount.

Technology Is the Future

Regardless of the industry, the future belongs to those dedicated to technology. Moore's Law favors the disciplined Finder who uses this law to take the company to new levels in the future.

Conversely, those Finders who avoid Moore's law and fail to budget money to comply with the law will be severely punished by the market and by the competition.

B2B truism: *The company that does not comply with Moore's law (i.e., invest in technology and computer infrastructure, regardless of the industry) will be severely punished by this law.*

CHAPTER 14

Bankers and Lenders Friends or Foes?

Most Finders view bankers and lenders as they do members of the opposite sex: They will spend a lifetime pursuing them, but feel they will never be able to understand or satisfy them.

Many Finders have a love-hate relationship with their bankers. They love the banker when they get enough money (at the right price) and hate them when they don't.

Finders spend too much time minding when it comes to the issue of bankers and lenders. They will spend many hours trying to find the right bank to get the company the right amount of money.

Bankers and lenders are critical to our economic society. Without them our economy would come to a screeching halt.

Obviously, bankers are not perfect. Just like people in any industry, there are good and bad bankers. Some bankers are the best their profession has to offer and others are an embarrassment to the banking and lending profession. The trick is to find the good ones and build long-term relationships with them for the future success of you and your company.

Increased Sales vs. Increased Cash Flow

Bankers want to know that your company is going in the right direction and has the tools to get you through The Danger Zone. I understand that you might get frustrated with a banker if your sales are going through the roof and the banker will not give you more money. Your banker understands that a *significant increase in sales will not necessarily mean an increase in cash flow.* In fact, the opposite is usually the norm.

B2B truism: *A significant increase in sales typically means the company might have a decrease in cash, which is the opposite of what Finders expect with high sales increases.*

The reason a growth company has less cash is because the cash is tied up in accounts receivable, payroll, inventory, fixed assets and other such items.

The Bank – Your Customer?

The best way to look at a bank is to try to pretend it is a customer of the company. What do you do for your customers? Well, you try to find out what they want so they will pay you money for your goods or services. You will spend weeks, months or even years trying to determine your customer's needs so they will give you money. Bankers can be viewed the same way. What do they want and what do you have to do to legally get their money?

Bankers want customers who:

- Issue clean interim financial statements on a timely basis
- File timely tax returns prepared by a reputable CPA
- Have an owner who understands the financial statements
- Invest in computer systems to help with internal controls
- Hire senior-level executives to help the Finder avoid minding activities
- Have acceptable key ratios
- Are going in the right direction

Naturally, you do not want to give too much away to the bank. Personal guarantees and other such items may have serious ramifications to you and your company. Again, find out what the bank needs and wants and plan a strategy with your senior-level advisors on how to get your cash at the best possible price.

Beat Them at Their Own Game

I have been in countless meetings where bankers have started to explain key ratios of a Finder's company only to see the Finder become disinterested or upset. Finders do not understand why bankers look at "old" data, such as the information on a balance sheet, to judge whether or not a company should receive a loan. Finders do not understand why bankers do not see into the Finder's future regarding the growth and opportunities of the company.

If you are frustrated, you are not playing the game the right way. In a sports analogy, you are letting the referees control the game. You should consider putting aside your feelings and beat the banker at his own game.

So, how is this done? How does a Finder beat the bank at its own game? The answers lie within the very nature of you as a Finder:

- Take control
- Lead
- Sell

There is no reason that you can't be prepared for the meeting with the bankers and have information prepared in advance to discuss with the banker. By information, I do not mean the typical information that Finders want to give bankers, such as projections, promises and estimates of the future. By information I mean:

- Correct financial statements
- Calculations of key ratios
- Interpretations of key ratios
- Simple projections with a list of assumptions

Key Ratios

You and your senior-level advisor can go to your favorite search engine and type in "financial ratios" to learn everything you need to know about this subject. Below are some key ratios and information you should consider documenting

in preparation for the meeting with your banker
(this list will vary by your industry):

- Working capital
- Current ratio
- Quick ratio
- Debt to equity ratio
- Days in accounts receivable
- Gross profit margin
- Inventory turnover ratio

What If I Have a Bad Current Ratio?

As a Finder, you can't afford to not know your
working capital amount and your current ratio.

Often the working capital and current ratios
are not where they should be to fulfill the cash
flow needs of the company and to meet banking
requirements. Some things to consider:

- Plan ways to take current debt to long-term
  debt.
- Look at ways to move related-party
  transactions in current liabilities to equity.
- Ask your banker for advice on this subject.
  Your banker will be impressed that you
  understand this topic and will most likely
  be eager to help you solve this problem.

Key ratios are best used if you have a two or three-year historical analysis with your current numbers.

EBITDA

You should be familiar with the EBITDA of your company. Calculate the amount and be prepared to discuss this with your banker. Below is some good information on this subject:

> "EBITDA is one of those terms that is increasingly used, but usually for the wrong reason. This article will define it and discuss how it can be useful, but also misleading.

> "EBITDA is an acronym for 'earnings before Interest, taxes, depreciation and amortization'. It is calculated by taking operating income and adding back to it depreciation and amortization expenses. EBITDA is used to analyze a company's operating profitability before non-operating expenses (such as interest and 'other' non-core expenses) and non-cash charges (depreciation and amortization).

115

The Good

"EBITDA can be used to analyze the profitability between companies and industries. Because it eliminates the effects of financing and accounting decisions, EBITDA can provide a relatively good 'apples-to-apples' comparison.

"The ratio can also be used to evaluate different industry trends over time. Because it removes the impact of financing large capital investments and depreciation from the analysis, EBITDA can be used to compare the profitability trends.

The Bad

"EBITDA is a good metric to evaluate profitability but not cash flow. Unfortunately, however, EBITDA is often used as a measure of cash flow, which is a very dangerous and misleading thing to do because there is a significant difference between the two.

The Ugly

"It gets ugly when EBITDA is used as a key measure for making investment decisions. Because it is easier to calculate, EBITDA is often used as a headline metric in discussing a company's results. This, however, could, as discussed above, misrepresent the true investment potential of a company because it does not accurately reflect a firm's ability to generate cash.

Conclusion

"EBITDA is a good measure to use to evaluate the core profit trends, but cash is king. EBITDA can be used to evaluate the profit potential between companies and industries because it eliminates some of the extraneous factors and allows a more 'apples-to-apples' comparison. But EBITDA should not replace the measure of cash flow, which includes the significant factor of changes in working capital. Cash is king because it shows 'true' profitability and a company's ability to continue operations."[23]

CHAPTER 15

Your Current and Future Different Customers

Your company's current customers are its life-blood. They bring the cash into the business and give everyone in the company a pay check.

While I could have included this information in Chapter 11, where I discussed The Danger Zone, I thought it important enough to warrant its own chapter. Finders *must* understand this topic in order to survive in the future.

As Finders, we spend a lot of time and money looking for and satisfying our customers. We then try to make them happy with our goods and services. We spend time collecting money in a manner that will not get them upset to the point they want to use one of our competitors.

Let's again review the graph that shows the Finder's transition to minding through the infrastructure changes discussed in previous chapters.

Finder Migration Stages

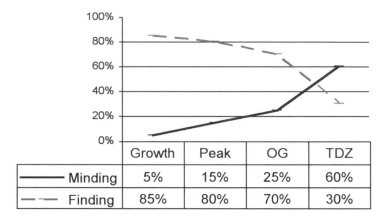

	Growth	Peak	OG	TDZ
—— Minding	5%	15%	25%	60%
— — Finding	85%	80%	70%	30%

The migration of a Finder into minding activities has a negative consequence as it relates to the current customers of the company. This migration has stages that all relate to the time and energy the Finder spends in minding activities. These stages are somewhat predictable, as follows:

Stage I	Distance
Stage II	Irritation
Stage III	Courting
Stage IV	Departure
Stage V	Sales Decrease
Stage VI	Change or Fold

Stage I   Distance

The Finder pulls back in quality and quantity time with the customer and is less visible to the customer. The Finder has desires to spend time with the customer and says things like, *"I'll give them a call next week."* Well, the next week passes and the weeks turn into months.

Stage II   Irritation

The customer does not understand the reason the Finder is creating distance. Consequently, the Finder becomes less important to the customer. The customer may begin to pay bills late, make short-pays, create change orders or do other things that irritate the Finder. The Finder, who is now more involved in minding activities, starts to harbor bad feelings toward the customer. In times past, the Finder would go see the customer, take him to dinner or on a golf outing and smooth things over. Today, the Finder feels compelled to stay in the office to handle the daily crisis. The Finder may shoot the customer a terse email or may send a subordinate to the customer to solve the problem. The relationship between the customer and the Finder weakens.

Stage III   Courting

Eventually, the customer leaks word to the Finders competition that the door may be open for a preliminary discussion. The competition jumps at the chance and does everything possible to steal the customer away. Sometimes the competitor fails, but all too often the competitor gets a foot in the door and starts a relationship with the Finder's customer. The wining and dining begins. Promises are made. Tempting proposals are presented. Meanwhile, the Finder is back at the office, buried in minding activities and totally unaware of the progress made by the competition.

Stage IV Departure

Time passes and the distance in the relationship between the Finder and the customer increases. The relationship between the customer and the Finder's competition starts to get warmer. Over time, the customer simply leaves the Finder to pursue greener pastures with the Finder's competition.

Stage V   Sales Decrease

As customers leave, the Finder spends even more time minding by managing cash and doing other day-to-day activities. Sales decrease. Cash flow becomes a problem. The company is headed in the wrong direction.

Stage VI Change or Fold

The Finder, realizing that customers are leaving, now has a couple of choices: (1) Let the company go out of business or (2) Hire someone to mind the business while the Finder goes out to do what he or she is trained to do – bring customers to the business. The success or failure of the company will depend upon (1) the ability of the Finder to bring in customers, and (2) the ability of the new Minder to hold down the fort and to find resources for the Finder to bring home the bacon. A good team effort *may* produce positive results.

The Future Different Customer

One of the dangers of Finders becoming Minders has to do with the subject of the company's Future Different Customers.

A Future Different Customer, in B2B terms, is not a new customer that would buy the goods or services that you sell today. Rather, the Future Different Customer is a customer that exists in the future who will possibly purchase goods and services that the Finder has not yet created. Here is an example:

I started my company in 1987, many years before the Internet was available to the consumer. In the beginning, I was the only person in the company. Today, my firm is a national company that serves most of the largest cities in the country.

The growth of my company is directly related to the concept of the Future Different Customer. The growth of my firm from one person to a nationwide firm is due largely to someone deciding a few years ago to create search engines on the Internet. The creation of search engines made it possible for potential customers to find my company's website simply by inputting key words into the search engine. Today, any individual can type in words such as CFO, Part-time CFO, and dozens of other terms. These words will lead people to my firm's website, www.b2bcfo.com, which gives us an opportunity to be connected with a potential customer.

In other words, someone did some *planning* a few years ago and conceived an idea to cause me to pay them money in lieu of paying money to typical advertising outlets such as newspapers, mailers, television, radio and so forth.

Brilliant thinking on their part? Absolutely. Has this forward-thinking by these people been beneficial to me and my company? Without question!

And so this topic relates to you. As a Finder you have two choices:

- You can get out of minding, begin to dream, invest in technology and begin to find new markets of Future Different Customers that will pay you money, or:

- You can sit back, spend time minding and let your competition find the Future Different Customers that might have been yours.

The Future Different Customers will be created and found *either by you or your competition*. The choice is yours and depends upon the discipline you have to spend time Finding. You need the time to dream, plan, visualize, research and "pull" others into the future.

B2B truism: *Someone is spending time with your current and future different customer. If not you, it will be your competition.*

CHAPTER 16

The Black Clouds that Haunt

It has been my experience that most Finders live 24/7, 365 with things that bother them about their business or businesses. The purpose of this chapter is to identify some of those concerns and to propose possible solutions.

Black Cloud #1 - April 15th

I was in Scottsdale last year having a meeting with a Finder who was a referral from a bank. We were enjoying a pleasant conversation discussing both of our companies. He was in an unique industry and was experiencing significant growth in his company.

During the conversation I asked a simple question, *"Do you receive accurate internal projections about the amount of money you will owe the IRS on April 15th?"*

His demeanor instantly changed. He became very agitated and said, *"Jerry, let me ask you a question. Why did my CPA make me write a check to the IRS for $138,000 last week when my company doesn't even make any money?"*

It has been my experience that Finders walk around 24/7, 365 with a black cloud related to the subject of income taxes. They either have had bad experiences, such as the one mentioned above or have heard about the bad experiences from colleagues. They know their company is growing and are expecting something bad when April 15th hits.

It has also been my experience to know there is no reason for a Finder to walk around with this April 15th black cloud. Income taxes are, after all, just math calculations. Mathematical calculations can be computed at any time, assuming the information being used is accurate.

B2B truism: *Many Finders spend too much energy worrying about the amount of money they will owe the IRS on April 15th.*

A Solution to April 15th

There is a solution to the April 15th problem. I'd like to suggest four steps for you to follow to resolve this issue. You will sleep better at night and can get rid of this black cloud if you delegate and make sure that competent people do the following:

1. Give you accurate financial statements
2. Give you timely financial statements
3. Calculate your income taxes monthly
4. Have the calculations verified quarterly from your independent CPA

Accurate Financial Statements

Moore's Law, discussed in Chapter 13, has significantly impacted this topic of accurate financial statements.

On the positive side, it has created opportunities for Finders to have very good computers and accounting software for a minimal cost. When I first started my career, a business owner might need to invest a six-figure amount in computer infrastructure for accounting hardware and software. Today, a Finder can purchase hardware and software to help run the business at a fraction of the cost that was required a few decades ago.

The bad news is that much of the accounting software that can be purchased today does not require skilled people to input financial information, such as cash disbursements, cash receipts, bills from vendors, etc.

A Finder's natural tendency is to invest as little cash as possible in this area. Consequently, we see people who input data into the Finder's computer with no idea if the information is correct or incorrect. We then see the classic effect of GIGO – garbage in, garbage out. Often we see accounting staff who have absolutely no clue as to whether or not the financial information is right or wrong. Sometimes we discover that accounting staff have over-stated their abilities when they interviewed for the job. Sometimes we determine that the accounting staff had the basic skills when the company first started but do not have the knowledge when the company is several times larger than when it was in its infancy.

We also see the complication of related-party transactions. Finders have a tendency to create multiple companies. The internal accounting staff typically can input data, but has no idea as to whether the data as it relates to the various entities is right or wrong.

B2B truism: *Your company must have accurate financial statements in order to make accurate projections of the income taxes that will be owed on April 15th.*

It is our recommendation that the Finder's financial statements be accurate each and every month of the year. It is the Finder's responsibility to hire the right people to ensure financial statement accuracy.

B2B truism: *Employees are often afraid to admit mistakes or to notify the Finder about bad news regarding the financial statements. These employees are concerned about their "job security" and will often not disclose bad news until it is absolutely imperative, even if the failure to disclose errors is to the detriment of the Finder.*

Timely Financial Statements

Your financial statements need to be issued monthly. Unless there is an unusual circumstance, the financial statements should be issued no later than the end of the next month.

Calculate Income Taxes Monthly

It is very simple to calculate income taxes monthly after you have timely and accurate financial statements.

Most closely held companies are pass-through entities for income tax reporting. That often means that income from one company can be offset with losses from another company, provided there is sufficient basis in the company that has incurred the loss. There are different rules for "basis" calculation for S-Corporations and LLCs, however the rules are simple to understand.

B2B truism: *Many Finders become very frustrated on April 15th because they discover, at the last moment, that the losses in one company can't be used to offset income in a different related-party company.*

You should be told, each month, the approximate amount of income taxes that will be owed on April 15th. You should then be able to know the amount of cash that needs to be set aside to pay your income taxes.

B2B truism: *There should be no negative surprises to a Finder on April 15th.*

Verification From Your Independent CPA

You should have your independent CPA verify the internally-projected income taxes at least once a quarter. This will give you some peace of mind regarding April 15th. This quarterly update should not cost much money if the internal financial statements are accurate and timely.

Black Cloud #2 – Decision Making

Finders, by personality trait, are quick decision makers. This is one of the attributes that sets them apart from others in our society. They quickly gather facts and use their intuition to make decisions. This is a good trait and is necessary for good leadership. This trait, however, can lead to disaster if the facts the Finder is using are erroneous.

Most Finders are of above-average in intelligence, regardless of their formal education. This being said, one must realize that it is highly probable that the Finder of one's competition is also above average in intelligence. In the long run, the goal is to make better decisions than the competition; otherwise, the Finder runs the risk of being beaten by the competitor. The question then becomes, "How does a Finder make better decisions than the competition?"

Regardless of your intelligence, you increase the probability of making a bad decision if the information you are using to make the decision is erroneous.

B2B truism: *Bad financial information typically leads to bad decision making.*

Conversely, you increase your probability of making good decisions if the information you are using to make the decision is correct. One of the reasons a Finder must invest in infrastructure is to be able to receive accurate and timely information from the accounting department. The risk is too great to cut corners on this important function.

B2B truism: *If you expect to beat your competition, you must have better financial information infrastructure than does your competition.*

Black Cloud #3 – Borrowing From the IRS

One of the joys I have experienced in life is waking up early in the morning at Lake Powell to witness the beauty of the lake before any boats or humans hit the surface. The view is stunning. The lake reflects the shapes and colors of the surrounding canyons like a piece of glass. After pondering the beauty of the surroundings, I typically pick up a stone and toss it into the lake. If I toss the stone out 20 feet or so, I can watch the ripple effect of my actions. Eventually, the impact of the stone will cause hundreds of rings to form around the point of impact. It is an interesting sight and gives me an opportunity to ponder upon life.

The above is analogous to another effect of Moore's Law, which was discussed in Chapter 13. The ripple effect of this law has caused an infusion of cheap accounting software into the business community. While often appearing advantageous, the improper usage of this software can turn into a disaster for the Finder.

We see too many companies that have their Minders cutting payroll checks from software packages owned by the Finder's business. This creates great potential for problems to arise in the following areas:

- Money must be paid timely to the IRS
- Possibility arises for theft by the Minder
- Forms 941 and 940 must be filed on time
- W-2's must be filed on time

All too often, the Minder does not do things correctly in these areas and the Finder is then responsible to the IRS and state governments for the errors caused by the Minder.

Another danger exists in this area as a company gets closer to The Danger Zone. Often, as a result of cash shortages, the Finder will make a decision to not pay the payroll taxes to the IRS. The initial idea by the Finder is to use this cash, on a temporary basis, to cover other cash flow problems. This often turns into a situation that is not easily reversed.

B2B truism: *Never borrow money from the IRS or any other governmental taxing authority.*

The Federal and State withholdings from your employees pay are typically called "Trust Funds." The government does not look favorably upon business owners who delay payments on trust funds. The penalties in terms of dollars can be significant. I have seen penalties ranging from 25% to 35%. Even worse, the government can charge the business owner with civil and criminal penalties. The cost is not worth the perceived benefit. Avoid borrowing from the government, at all costs.

The payroll processing wheel has been invented. There are multi-billion dollar companies that can process your payroll on a cost-effective basis. They can also provide your company with current human resource manuals that can help guide you though the complicated issues related to human resources.

B2B truism: *Concentrate on your company's core competencies and avoid re-inventing the payroll and human resources wheels.*

Pitfalls of Internal Payroll Processing

Some of the pitfalls of payroll processing and human resource management include:

- Penalties for late payments
- Fair Labor Standards Act compliance
- Accounting creating fictitious employees
- Errors in withholdings
- Family Medical Leave Act compliance
- Recordkeeping
- Changes in reporting due to errors
- Employee vs. independent contractor laws
- Sexual harassment lawsuits and compliance
- Unemployment compensation issues
- Wage garnishments

- Workers compensation issues
- Minimum wage compliance for a sales force
- Domestic service compliance
- COBRA compliance

RECORDKEEPING

The Fair Labor Standards Act requires employers to keep the following records:

"Every employer covered by the Fair Labor Standards Act (FLSA) must keep certain records for each covered, nonexempt worker. There is no required form for the records, but the records must include accurate information about the employee and data about the hours worked and the wages earned. The following is a listing of the basic records that an employer must maintain:

- Employee's full name, as used for social security purposes, and on the same record, the employee's identifying symbol or number if such is used in place of a name on any time, work, or payroll records;
- Address, including zip code;
- Birth date, if younger than 19;
- Sex and occupation;
- Time and day of week when employee's workweek begins. Hours worked each day

and total hours worked each workweek;
- Basis on which employee's wages are paid;
- Regular hourly pay rate;
- Total daily or weekly straight-time earnings;
- Total overtime earnings for the workweek;
- All additions to, or deductions from, the employee's wages;
- Total wages paid each pay period;
- Date of payment and the pay period covered by the payment."[24]

Payroll recordkeeping is too complicated to try to cut corners or to handle internally. Eventually, the internal accounting or human resource department will make an error. The error could be significant and is not worth the risk. The hiring of a payroll processing company does not mean a Finder needs to lose control of payroll. If you wish, you can still sign checks. You do not need to have the entire payroll (net checks) taken out of your account in one lump sum.

B2B truism: *Use a payroll company to build your payroll and human resource infrastructure.*

Black Cloud #4 – Overtime

There are few companies that do not make errors in overtime calculations. The penalties for making errors in overtime can be severe and can cause much damage to a company.

Overtime is governed by the Fair Labor Standards Act (FLSA) and was approved by Congress in 1938. It is stunning to me that a law created so long ago is so little known or understood by Finders today.

It is not unusual for me to be hired by a company and to discover that the company is in violation of the FLSA. The violation is often in the form of paying a person a "salary." When bringing the issue up to a Finder, the response is typically that the person does not get paid overtime because they are on a salary. Finders often become frustrated when I explain that there are rules that require payment of overtime, even if a person is being paid a salary.

B2B truism: *A company may be responsible for overtime, even if an employee is being paid a salary.*

There are certain exemptions for executive, administrative, professional, outside sales and computer employees, however; the reasons for those exemptions must be known and documented.

There are also rules that require overtime with a commissioned sales staff. The rules are somewhat complicated but are not worth the risk of violating.

The FLSA has made the following statement:

"An employer who requires or permits an employee to work overtime is generally required to pay the employee premium pay for such overtime work. Employees covered by the Fair Labor Standards Act (FLSA) must receive overtime pay for hours worked in excess of 40 in a workweek of at least one and one-half times their regular rates of pay."[25]

I have participated with numerous Department of Labor (DOL) audits during my career. Typically, I have been brought into the argument after the overtime laws have been allegedly violated. I have discovered that the DOL laws, while complicated, are documented very well. I have observed through numerous meetings with the DOL that they try to be fair but are not flexible.

I remember a wrap-up meeting with the DOL on a particular engagement. They thoroughly explained the fines and penalties. They also explained the time-frame for which the monies had to be paid. They surprised the business owner with a large fine that was in addition to the other monies that were assessed. The business owner got very upset and pleaded his case, but did not change the mind of the DOL auditor. After the business owner left the room I asked the auditor why the DOL was issuing the fine. I will never forget the answer, which was, *"Jerry, this law has been in place since 1938 and the owner should have taken the responsibility to know the law."*

B2B truism: *The Department of Labor is powerful. Their laws, some of which were enacted in 1938, should be understood and complied with by the business owner.*

Black Cloud #5 – Control

Few things bother a Finder more than feeling a loss of control over the company. Finders who own growth companies sometimes feel as if they are steering a large ship without a rudder.

The feeling of loss of control typically results from failure to build a proper infrastructure. Some of the infrastructure areas that cause the most frustrations are:

- Accounting
- Computer hardware and software
- Website designs
- Record keeping
- Back-up of data

Here's my advice. Never relinquish control of important infrastructure areas. This does not mean you should be a micro-manager of these areas. It does mean that you should hire the best people available so that you can trust what they are doing for your company. Regarding accounting and accounting records, I have some suggestions:

- Don't outsource your accounting. Create an infrastructure where the accounting is done on-site with accounting software that you own and that is secure within your environment. Have a computer in your office and have someone teach you how to access critical data in your company. Your employees need to know you are looking over their shoulders. You do not need to become an accounting expert. Rather, hire someone who can give you the power to get to your information at any time you wish, even if the access is remote via a laptop.

• Don't let important documents leave your company. There is no reason to let important documents (check registers, etc) leave the company premises. The problem with outsourcing accounting is the Finder often has to let key documents leave the office. Don't let this happen. Rather, make sure you know where the key documents are located. Let your accounting staff know that you can go to the files and look at key documents at any time. Let a professional teach you how to do this if you do not know what to look for in your company. This will not only give you a feeling of control but will also send a serious message to your staff.

- Make a soft-copy back-up of key data. Create an infrastructure environment in which key documents are scanned and saved on your file servers.

- Have someone other than your accounting department open the bank statements.

- Require a test of your back-up procedures. Require your staff to periodically show you the backup. Do not trust that it is going to get done. Be in control of this area and require people to show you the back-up data.

B2B truism: *A Finder should never relinquish control over the company.*

Black Cloud #6 – Being Held Hostage

Invariably, when engaged with a company, I will sit down with the Finder and explain that certain employees have the ability to hold the company hostage. This means that certain employees have so much knowledge or so many responsibilities that, if they were to leave the company, the act of leaving would cause serious harm to the company. I have seen employees who, understanding this hostage-holding issue, have created situations where he or she has negotiated salary and benefits that exceed the market for their particular skills. This is hostage-taking by the employee of the Finder and the Finder is often afraid of reprimanding, terminating or disciplining the employee because of possible repercussions to the company.

The keys to correcting this situation are to (1) identify the potential hostage-holding situation and (2) hire someone to create an infrastructure around the situation. In other words, internal controls and other systems need to be put in place so that the company can continue to function if the person was to leave the company, either voluntarily or involuntarily.

B2B truism: *Hostage-holding by one of your employees, whether voluntary or involuntary, is detrimental to any company.*

Black Cloud #7 – The Balance Sheet

I truly enjoy visiting with Finders. I become motivated by their intelligence, their drive and their ambitions.

One of the peculiar things about a Finder is that they can always tell me their personal net worth.

If we are talking over lunch about this subject, the Finder can grab a napkin and write his or her net worth on the napkin in a few minutes. They know the value of their homes, the mortgage and the other assets they own. They have a keen ability to keep numbers in their heads and know their major personal assets and liabilities.

On the other hand, for some reason, Finders react differently when I bring up the subject of the company's balance sheet. Finders typically tell me things such as, *"I don't understand the balance sheet,"* or *"I see no reason to look at the balance sheet,"* or *"I know the balance sheet is wrong, so there is no reason for me to get involved,"* or *"The balance sheet is not important to me because it does not show the true value of my assets."*

There are numerous reasons why you need to understand your company's balance sheet. A few of the key reasons are:

- The assets and liabilities of the company are on this page. It is very important for you to understand what the company owns in assets and what it owes in debts.

- It is highly likely that a weak accounting infrastructure or weak accounting staff will cause errors on the balance sheet. It is important for you to be able to tell people that you know about the errors and that you want the errors fixed. A Finder who does not understand the balance sheet runs the risk of employee theft and other detrimental issues.

- Your banker will closely analyze your company's balance sheet and will create key ratios mostly from the balance sheet. You want to be able to communicate your understanding of the balance sheet and ratios to your banker. A Finder who is able to converse with a banker about the balance sheet will not only gain respect from the banker but will also be able to negotiate and understand banker's terms.

- The balance sheet shows the equity you have in the company. You should know how much equity you have in your company, just as you know the equity you have in your home.

B2B truism: *The Finder must understand the company's balance sheet.*

Black Cloud #8 – Employee Pay

The proper amount to pay an employee is a frustrating topic to Finders. There often seems to be no middle ground on this topic. Business owners often feel they are over-paying employees and search for rules or guidelines for pay. One can go on any search engine to find grades of recommended pay for employees. These published grades of pay are usually meaningless.

A simple rule of thumb can be used to determine the amount an employee should be paid: Find the amount of money it will take to replace and train the employee. Unless unusual circumstances occur, the company's employees should not be paid above market value.

B2B truism: *Employee pay is dictated by the market.*

B2B truism: *An employee who is paid above market will eventually leave the company.*

There are a few reasons that an employee who is being paid above market will eventually leave the company:

- The Finder knows the employee is being over paid. This fact is always in the back of the Finders mind. Eventually, this will bother the Finder enough that a situation will be created to cause the employee to leave the company.

- An employee knows when he is being over paid and is smart enough to know when a Finder is creating an infrastructure that will expose the inflated salary. When this infrastructure creation is near completion, the employee will often go out and find a job with a different company in lieu of being asked to take a pay cut. Sometimes, the employee leaves to work for a competitor.

Pay your employees what the market will bear, and nothing more than that amount. There is nothing wrong with giving periodic bonuses to reward outstanding or exceptional behavior. Any bonus given to an employee should acknowledge that (1) the bonus is for a specific event or period of time and (2) any future bonuses will be discretionary and may or may not occur.

Black Cloud #9 – Statement of Cash Flows

The company's statement of cash flows is typically the financial statement document that the Finder least understands. This is an unfortunate situation because the statement of cash flows is often the *most important document* the Finder can use to run a company.

The premise behind the statement of cash flows is very simple: It begins with the year-to-date profit or loss and shows the specific areas where cash has increased or decreased.

While the premise of this document is simple, the practical application is very complicated. The form itself, as dictated by GAAP (Generally Accepted Accounting Principles) is inadequate.

That being said, the Finder *must* understand the statement of cash flows. There are ways, assuming you surround yourself with the right people, that you can understand this document. Once you understand the statement, you can use it to run the company and be more in control of cash.

A simple way to determine if you need more help with this subject is to have your existing staff explain the statement of cash flows to you. You are in good shape if you sense confidence from the staff and if you can understand the document with the staff's explanation. The opposite response should give you cause to consider bringing in someone else to help with the matter.

B2B truism: *A Finder can't run the risk of not understanding the Statement of Cash Flows.*

Finders: There is no reason to have any of the black clouds described in this chapter follow or haunt you. Get rid of them and enjoy life a little more.

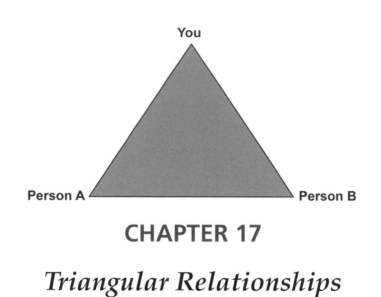

Person A   Person B

CHAPTER 17

Triangular Relationships

I'll start this chapter by acknowledging that I may step on some toes with this topic.

I am going to share this information with the hope that it will help you with the topic of triangular relationships, which will occur in your business, whether or not you create them on purpose.

B2B truism: *Finders create triangular relationships.*

As a consultant to Finders, this is a subject that causes me a lot of frustration. It also causes a lot of frustration to your employees and, if not controlled, can damage key relationships.

I did not learn about triangular relationships in college, but from a business physiologist in the mid 1980s. I was sharing some frustrations about business when he began to chuckle. I told him that I did not find this issue particularly amusing. He continued to chuckle and said, *"Jerry, you are caught in the middle of a triangular relationship."* He then patiently taught me about the subject. He also taught me how to get out of the middle of triangular relationships, which has been an important reason for my business success.

Relationships

Webster defines a relationship as, *"A state of affairs existing between those having shared dealings."*

The adage *"It's not what you know but who you know"* is one of the best jewels of wisdom of the ages.

The best Finders are those who know how to build long-term relationships. Those relationships are typically the foundation of the finding activities, as discussed previously in this book. A business relationship typically starts between two people and looks like the following:

You ⟷ Person A

You and Person A spend time together in a mutually beneficial business relationship. As is the case with all relationships, there is some give-and-take as you both work toward your mutual goals, which may or may not be self-serving in nature.

A Triangular Relationship

A triangular relationship occurs when a third person is brought into the relationship with you and Person A. This relationship of the three of you now looks something like the following:

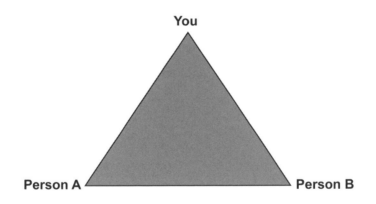

So far, there is nothing wrong with the relationship among the three of you. You all work well together, the lines of communication are open and there is a mutually-beneficial and healthy business relationship among the three parties. This relationship works as long as the communication lines look something like the following:

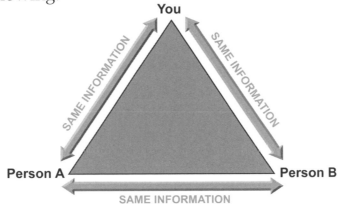

The trouble begins when the communications among the three parties breaks down and one or more legs of the triangle become imbalanced. The imbalance is typically caused by either (1) not communicating or (2) by communication of different information among the three parties. The communication lines then start to look something like the following, with multiple variables.

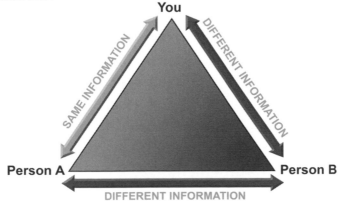

An Example – The Family

"Dad comes home from work to find Mom coming down hard on Junior with, "Clean up your room or else," threats. He (Dad) immediately comes to the rescue. "Mom," he might say, "Give the boy a break." Perhaps Mom, feeling victimized by Dad, turns on him, automatically moving in to a victim position. They might do a few quick trips around the triangle with Junior on the sidelines. Or maybe Junior joins Dad in a persecutory, "Let's gang up on Mom" approach, and they could play it from that angle. Or Junior could turn-coat on Dad, rescuing Mom, with: "Mind your own business, Dad ... I don't need your help!" So it goes, with endless variations perhaps, but nonetheless, round and round the triangle."[26]

As parents, we all most likely have inadvertently created a similar triangular relationship between our spouse and our children. Husbands, at least the smart ones, quickly learn this is a losing position to take.

And so it goes in business. Finders create triangular relationships that cause harm to the business, just as such relationships cause harm to families and family members.

Let's discuss a couple of the most common types of this phenomenon in business, multiple owners of a closely held company and nepotism.

Co-owners of a Business

Co-owners cause triangular relationships with employees, vendors, bankers, customers and a host of people. This sometimes occurs in situations such as the following:

- The co-owners do not have the same information. The source of information and the methods of communications between co-owners are critical. They must have identical information from accounting, vendors, bankers, employees, customers, etc. They must also meet often to discuss the information received from the variety of sources to make sure they comprehend the information in the same way between the owners. Otherwise, they take the risk of creating triangular relationships.

- The co-owners do not like, trust or respect each other. Often, co-owners become irritated with each other. Sometimes, the irritation leads to a deterioration of the relationship. This situation is bad when the change in relationship is understood between the co-owners. This situation becomes dangerous when only one of the co-owners understands the change in the relationship. What occurs in this case is Owner A will start communicating with other people instead of talking with Owner B. We then have the following triangular relationship:

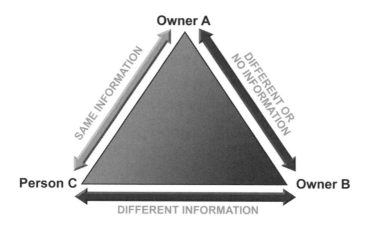

This is a dangerous situation!

No possible good will result from this change in relationships. This is not only a lose-lose for the owners but puts Person C in an insecure situation. Person C is forced to start "taking sides" with one of the owners. Owner A will typically go to Person C and say something such as, *"Don't tell Owner B, but I have decided to ...."*

In this situation, Owner A is not only looking out for his or her own best interest but is putting Person C in a precarious situation. The Person Cs of the world, if they are employees of the company, often become stressed over this type of a change in the triangular relationship. They often feel like they are asked to lie or keep secrets. They then go home and spend time discussing this situation with their spouse and/or other people. They feel they are painted into a corner and start to worry if they will get in trouble with Owner B.

Another danger of the above example is that Person C (employee, vendor, banker, customer, etc.) often begins to question the judgment of Owner A. He often thinks or says to himself (or others) something like, *"Well, if Owner A is going to do this to one of his partners, I wonder when he or she is going to do the same to me."* Person C's self-defense mechanisms then kick in. Person C starts to withdraw from both Owner A and Owner B. Person C hopes that Owner A will stop sharing this information and, simultaneously, hopes that Owner B will never discover the "secret" that has been shared. Person C has unnecessary burdens placed upon his or her back. These burdens are bothersome, stressful and eventually take a toll. The toll may not be worth the cost to Owner A or Owner B.

B2B truism: *Co-owners should communicate with each other or end the relationship.*

There are only two solutions to correct the communication lines between two co-owners:

- They agree to communicate with each other, in spite of their changed feelings: Or,

- They agree to end the relationship by creating an exit strategy for one of the owners.

Nepotism

Nepotism is a peculiar source of triangular relationships that often causes damage in a company.

Webster tells us the word is derived from the Latin word nepot and is defined as: *"Favoritism shown to a relative (as by giving an appointive job.)"*

I can guarantee you that most of your employees regard the word "nepotism" as a four-letter word, although they will never say this to your face. The nepotism triangular relationship looks something like the following:

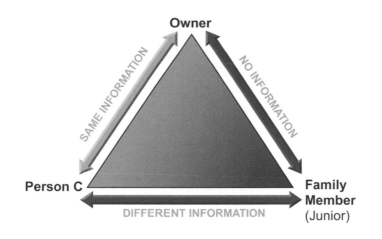

The trouble with hiring a family member is that person C assumes nepotism exists, whether or not that is the case. The owner will typically try to avoid any conflict with Junior and will sit down with Person C and demand that he or she confront Junior. This puts Person C in a bad situation because Person C is smart enough to know the adage, *"Blood is thicker than water"* and assumes that bad things are going to occur.

A simple way to explain the problem with this situation is to describe a peculiar weakness that Finders have in running their business – that of delegating responsibilities without giving authority.

Responsibility vs. Authority

Finders are good at delegating responsibilities. This is a natural part of their personalities and is a key component of what makes them a Finder.

B2B truism: *Finders are good at delegating responsibility but bad at giving authority.*

So we quickly get to the root of the problem with nepotism. The Finder delegates to Person C the responsibility to shape up Junior without giving the *authority* to person C to fire or reprimand Junior.

Person C knows he or she has been given the responsibility but *not* the authority, creating a lose-lose situation between Person C and the owner. Person C's self-defense mechanisms kick into gear. This person begins to sugar-coat instructions with Junior hoping that Junior will not go home and tell Mom or Dad that Person C has been unfair. Person C knows that Junior is not above lying to Mom or Dad to keep the job. In fact, Person C suspects that Junior is good at playing Mom and Dad against each other. Hence, we often see a double triangular relationship that looks like the following:

The Owner vs. Person C vs. Junior
and / or
Mom vs. Person C vs. Junior

Fellow employees begin to talk or laugh behind the back of the owner and / or Junior. Employees begin to let Junior "slide through the rules" of the company with the hope that they will not be reprimanded by Junior's Mom or Dad.

B2B truism: *Nepotism should be avoided at all costs. Family members should be treated like any other employee.*

No good can result from showing favoritism to a family member. Following are some potential consequences:

- The owner is harmed because Junior does not learn the discipline necessary to become a productive adult.

- Junior does not learn the skills necessary to lead the company in the future.

- Junior does not earn the respect of the employees of the company and becomes unqualified to lead the company in the future.

- Employees become demoralized by nepotism and lose respect for both the owner and the family member.

- Key employees begin to look for an exit strategy to avoid Junior and the future confrontations that will likely occur.

B2B truism: *Family members should perform better for the company than regular employees. Family members should be fired if they perform below average.*

At a minimum, should you choose to employ family members, pay them the going market rate for their services.

Get Out of Triangular Relationships

The intelligent person will recognize a triangular relationship and will voluntarily leave the relationship. A good way to do this is to sit down with the party that is causing the triangular relationship and calmly express the desire to be removed from the relationship. If this does not work, you might need to consider removing yourself from the relationship permanently. Let me give you an example.

I was hired a few years ago by the personal representative of a man who had been brutally murdered. The personal representative became the defacto CEO of the company owned by the murdered person. The company was in multiple states and had between 80 and 100 employees.

The new CEO and I worked together for a couple of years to try to save the company. Sadly, the company had been left with too much debt. (There was a key-man life insurance policy, but it went to a family member, not the company.) Eventually, the weight of personal and company debt left the defacto CEO no choice but to file Chapter 11 bankruptcy.

When the company filed Chapter 11 the court gave the secured creditors a significant amount of power to control the destiny of the company. The power of the secured creditors exceeded the power of the defacto CEO. A meeting was eventually held with the attorneys and other representatives of the secured creditors and the defacto CEO. I attended the meeting against my will. The representatives of the secured creditors began to make demands of me that were simply not acceptable to me. I could very easily provide the information requested; however, the relationship changed to the degree that I was put in a position to report to the secured creditors instead of the defacto CEO. I immediately saw the triangular relationship that was about to form. I saw a win-lose-lose relationship, with the secured creditor as the only winner. I abruptly left the meeting and resigned. In that situation, I did not create the triangular relationship but had the power to remove myself from the situation. I exercised my power and did not look back.

Do yourself a favor: Recognize when you are in or are creating triangular relationships. Then, either stop or remove yourself from the triangular relationship.

B2B truism: *There is never a win-win-win in a bad triangular relationship. The only permanent solution is to fix or remove oneself from such a situation.*

CHAPTER 18

An Exit Strategy

I have been a professional since 1978 and have seen more about business succession than I ever imagined I would see when I was in college at Arizona State University. I have seen the mergers and acquisitions. I have seen the forced sales of companies due to bad management or employee theft. I have seen the sale of companies because of the death of the owner, both by disease and by murder. There have been so many variables in business succession that I have concluded there are only two constants:

B2B truism: *Either you will outlive your company or your company will outlive you.*

You might consider an exit strategy from your company, regardless of which of the two above situations will occur. A planned exit strategy is better than an unplanned one. An unplanned exit strategy typically causes an untimely death to the company by means of liquidation, bankruptcy or other means.

Below are a few of the possibilities with a planned exit strategy:

- Sell the business to a third party
- Sell the business to a family member
- Stop the business and convert assets to cash
- Sell the business to employees
- Plan for your untimely death by the company paying the spouse or estate a certain amount of money that is funded by an insurance policy.

Building vs. Exiting Strategies

Finders are typically so busy creating or building the company that they do not have the inclination to work on the exit strategy. As we discussed above, *there will be an exit* of the Finder from the company, either voluntarily or involuntarily. The prudent business owner will begin to work on an exit strategy that is as seamless and well planned as possible.

Where to Start

The Finder needs to start cultivating relationships with people that can help create the exit strategy. These people typically are:

- Estate planning attorneys
- CPAs who specialize in exit strategies
- Business valuation experts
- Insurance experts
- Infrastructure creation experts

Preliminary discussions on your long-term exit strategies should begin with an estate planning attorney and a CPA. A Finder does not need to feel compelled to have a plan quickly documented. Rather, you can hold annual meetings to allow a plan or plans to grow to fit your needs or desires. Knowledge is power and a Finder can gather knowledge about the exit strategy over a period of time. Do not rule out getting a second opinion if you do not understand the input from your team. Discuss this subject with other successful business owners to get their input and advice.

Build Value Through Infrastructure

Let's assume you choose one or more of the three possible exit strategies:

- Sell the business to a third party
- Sell the business to a family member
- Sell the business to employees

B2B truism: *The less dependency upon key people, especially the owner, the more value will be assigned to a company upon an arms-length transaction sale.*

Let's refer back to what has become, I'm sure, one of your all-time favorite phrases, *infrastructure building*. Perhaps you should consider the importance of infrastructure building to your exit strategy, *even if you dismiss all of the benefits discussed in previous chapters of this book.*

The next few pages are excepts from an article I was asked to write on this subject that was published in Strategies Magazine in August 2007 (www.strategies.com).

"Begin with the End in mind," is a saying made popular by Stephen R. Covey. This is wise advice and should be adhered to by every business owner.

One of the attributes of entrepreneurs is that of being a visionary. Keeping that in mind, it is prudent to begin a vision of a successful exit strategy from your company, since that end is inevitable.

I started my business in 1987. Like many entrepreneurs, in the beginning, "the End" was a tremendous effort to make enough money to feed my family. The End for me was to try to convince future customers they should pay me a fair price for what I was trying to sell.

The End was struggling through the frustrations of being a pioneer in a new industry and the frustration of learning new skills to explain my vision to people that I felt needed my services. In the beginning, there were many times that I felt the End might be the failure of my business, my vision and aspirations. I know that many entrepreneurs feel the same way at the outset of their business endeavors.

It is no longer a struggle to meet the financial needs of my family. A business concept that was new and revolutionary in 1987 is now well accepted in our business society and is easy to explain.

So, with credibility, I can discuss with my fellow entrepreneurs a new vision of the End - one with a successful exit strategy - one that is planned, effective and beneficial to everyone. Well, beneficial to everyone except the competition!

Think Like A Buyer

If your exit strategy is to sell the business - whether to a third party, family members or employees – planning how to maximize your income by the sale of your business is essential.   Let's assume you wish to sell the company in the future at a good fair market value, regardless of who might purchase your business. What are some of the things you can start planning to make this a reality?

Discussing the sale of an entrepreneur's business is a very interesting exercise. Most business owners are very adamant about the amount of money they want for the business and are usually reluctant to accept any outside critique that might conflict with their dollar amount.

Regardless of your feelings about the value of your business, it will most likely be sold using a factor times your company's EBITDA (Earnings before Interest, Taxes, Depreciation and Amortization), averaged over a period of time. The information on this subject is easy to obtain and won't be discussed in this article. Rather, I prefer to help you take a step back and look at the big picture regarding the future value of your company. I'd like to share with you some ideas about the future value of your company in a way that perhaps nobody has suggested. The easiest way for me to help you with this subject is to have you assume that you are going to buy a business. Let's forget about your business for a while as you consider the following scenario, which will ultimately lead you to a better picture of how to improve the value of your own company.

Pretend that you are the buyer and are interested in purchasing a company. The seller's industry is different from the ones with which you are familiar, but the future of making money with this company looks very promising. The potential purchase of this company meets your goals to diversify your own existing business.

You meet with the owner, talk to some of the customers, meet some of the employees and are very excited about the transaction. You have a CVA (Certified Valuation Appraiser) give you a document verifying that the asking price is fair.

You talk about the transaction with your banker. The banker is supportive and agrees to advance money at a reasonable interest rate to help you make the purchase. Everything looks good on paper and feels good in your gut.

Just to be safe, you have a trusted senior-level executive look over the transaction prior to closing the deal. This person also feels good about the purchase, but brings to your attention certain issues that you have not considered so far in the transaction:

- The customers of the company do business solely based upon the close relationship they have with the company's owner.

- The company's computer hardware is being held together by the owner's brother-in law on "fix it when it breaks" approach. Some of the employees complain that the computer and telephone systems crash several times a month. Data is typically lost when the computers crash.

  The file servers, routers and other company hardware will need to be upgraded or replaced unless the new owner wants to risk a lot of possible down-time with the computer system. It is likely this will cost the new owner six-figures in investment.

- It is possible there will be liabilities for past services to customers; however, the data base the seller uses is unreliable and the estimated warranty issues are not known. You discuss this situation with the current owner. His reply is "I'll take care of things." You, however, have a nagging feeling in your gut telling you this might lead to possible future relationship problem with the company's customers.

- The procedures to build the goods or deliver the service are not documented in writing. Your advisor raises concern that the knowledge needed to create and deliver goods is merely in the minds of a few key employees. There is no guarantee these people will stay after the sale of the company. In fact, the current owner tells you that a couple of key people will bolt when they hear about the business being\ sold.

- The selling company has about 50 personal computers, most of which have multiple versions of illegal software. Your advisor tells you that very few of the computers have the same version of the same software, regardless of the possible issue of software piracy. It is estimated it will cost between $70,000 and $100,000 to correct this problem.

- There is no documentation regarding the intellectual property of the selling company. Doubts are raised by your advisor as to the authority of the selling company to transfer legal rights to these assets. There are also doubts about whether or not the seller legally owns the intellectual property claimed in the sales agreement and Web site.

- There is really no way to verify the accuracy of the numbers presented by the selling company's accounting department. The software is antiquated or corrupted. The conversion of data to a new system and or the buyer's existing system is doubtful. It is estimated that any conversion or reliability upon the seller's accounting data will take months to accomplish, as well as a six-figure investment.

- The current owner is working seven days a week and almost 15 hours a day to keep the company going. He has agreed to stay with you for a period of time after the sale to help with the transition. He also wants to take a couple of months off after you give him the check. Your advisor does a little homework and estimates that it

might take three people
commanding six-figure salaries
to replace all of the work being
performed by the current
owner.

Start Planning Your Exit Now

With these facts in mind, what are
you going to do now as the potential
purchaser of this company? You and
I already know the answer. You are
going to take the suggested sales
price and start subtracting dollars
from that amount.

My guess is, from the little
information disclosed above, you will
subtract a good seven-figure amount
from the sales price. Furthermore, you
will have justification to go back to
the seller to explain why the company
is now no longer worth the amount
previously discussed - even if your
banker has given you the green light
to go forward.

With the information you now have,
there is nothing in this world that

is going to convince you to pay the original sales price. In fact, you may decide that you no longer want to buy the business.

It is now time to look at the potential future sales price of your company. What do you think will happen to the future asking price of your company should a buyer become aware of your infrastructure failures or weaknesses before the close of the transaction? Well, we know the answer to that question: The buyer will either demand a lower price or will walk away from the deal.

Today is the day to start planning for the sale of your company. Start planning to hire key people if you do not have the time to document certain items. You might need to bring in some senior-level people to organize and document your systems, sometimes known as infrastructure or internal controls. You may want to consider having certified audits performed on your company's financial statements.

Start asking your key employees to document their activities, with the assumption that someone else might fill their position without doing any damage to the company. Have an independent company take a critical look at your company's computer hardware and software. You might be unpleasantly surprised at the amount of illegal software on your systems.

We can agree that this activity is expensive and time consuming. It is not nearly as expensive, however, as the missed opportunity for selling your company for a fair price in the future. You have the choice now: Start planning and creating value for your future exit strategy, or be prepared for a future purchaser to have ammunition to lower your suggested sales price. The wise will do the former.

B2B truism: *The better the infrastructure, the higher the probability an owner has to increase a sales price of a company.*

Exit by Death

Our Maker created all of us who are born into this life with a future expiration date. You can plan for an untimely exit from your company with good insurance. Some things you might consider are:

- The IRS may require an appraisal should you leave behind a company that has value. There may be federal or state taxes to be paid, depending upon the combined valuation of your company and other estate assets. Your advisors should help you with this planning. Be aware of certain "sunset" laws that may pop up in the future on certain estate taxes.

- Be sure to pay your life insurance premiums in a manner that will cause them to be tax free to the beneficiaries upon receipt. Question your tax advisors about this subject and double-check their work to ensure that life insurance proceeds will not be subject to income taxes.

- Ensure that the beneficiaries of any life insurance proceeds are those people that you wish to have receive them. I have witnessed the disaster that happens to a company and a family when the proceeds have been directed to someone other than the people the owner wished upon the owner's death. It would be wise to have a visit with your financial planners and insurance planners on this subject on a periodic basis.

CHAPTER 19

B2B CFO® Truisms

You have undoubtedly noticed the many B2B truisms listed in the previous chapters. Webster defines a truism as "an obvious truth." Well, these items are obviously truthful to me. You may not have liked or agreed with all of them. I would expect, however, that some of these truisms gave you pause to think and ponder.

For your quick reference, this chapter is a recap of all the B2B CFO® truisms from this book. You are encouraged to read them again and ponder.

FROM CHAPTER 1

Mission statements are often interesting but are not critical to a company's success.

You can't teach values, but you can find people who share your core values.

You want to get rid of anyone in your organization who does not share your core values. You also want those people to be hired by your competition. You will smile and consider

it a victory when your competitor hires your
former associates or employees who do not share
your core values, regardless of their skills.

If you delegate responsibility without the
authority, you will after a period of time, be
given back the responsibility.

Whether written or unwritten, the company's
organization chart exists today. The Finder's
future success is dependent upon working
properly within the rules of the informal
organization chart.

FROM CHAPTER 2

It is lonely at the top. Don't expect anyone to
understand or empathize with that loneliness.

FROM CHAPTER 3

Finders live in the future with little regard to
what has happened in the past.

Successful Finders are good relationship
builders.

Finders evoke strong emotions from others, such
as love or hate. There is no reason to try to be

friends with everyone, because they are looking for a leader, not a friend.

FROM CHAPTER 4

Minders live in the past and are not future thinkers.

Finders are not good Minders.

FROM CHAPTER 5

Most Finders started their careers as Grinders.

Grinders are only concerned about what happened today. No concern is given to the past or the future.

FROM CHAPTER 6

Far too many white-collar crimes committed by Minders are not reported to the authorities, which allows the Minder to steal from future employers.

We often find that many business owners unintentionally place their employees in a position to steal from the company.

FROM CHAPTER 7

Do not rely upon your CPA firm to detect theft or fraud, unless you specifically engage them for this function.

FROM CHAPTER 8

Most Finders do not spend a lot of time planning their business infrastructure.

FROM CHAPTER 10

Long-term planning takes time, money and discipline from the Finder.

The failure to plan infrastructure will eventually hurt the company and will take away time from finding customers at some point in the future.

Your competitors are actively planning today to take away your customers tomorrow.

FROM CHAPTER 11

The Danger Zone is when the cash needs of your company far exceed the cash available to meet those needs.

We have yet to see a Finder start a business so he can spend his time on accounting and computer problems, yet far too many spend too much time doing those things.

The Finder must learn to trust people. Employees should be terminated from the company if they are not trustworthy.

Good management is the accomplishment of the goals and objectives of the company through the actions of other people.

FROM CHAPTER 12

During TDZ, the Finder finds sales and the senior-level executives of the company find cash.

Leaders make tough decisions. There is no benefit in shuffling chairs on the deck of the Titanic. Leaders look to the future and avoid the icebergs that are in the path of their company.

FROM CHAPTER 13

Computers 4.5 years from now will be three times faster than computers you purchase today, which means you must have an active computer replacement plan.

The company that does not comply with Moore's law (i.e., invest in technology and computer infrastructure, regardless of the industry) will be severely punished by this law.

FROM CHAPTER 14

A significant increase in sales typically means the company might have a decrease in cash, which is the opposite of what Finders expect with high sales increases.

FROM CHAPER 15

Someone is spending time with your current and future different customer. If not you, it will be your competition.

FROM CHAPTER 16

Many Finders spend too much energy worrying about the amount of money they will owe the IRS on April 15th.

Your company must have accurate financial statements in order to make accurate projections of the income taxes that will be owed on April 15th.

Employees are often afraid to admit mistakes or to notify the Finder about bad news regarding the financial statements. These employees are concerned about their "job security" and will often not disclose bad news until it is absolutely imperative, even if the failure to disclose errors is to the detriment of the Finder.

Many Finders become very frustrated on April 15th because they discover, at the last moment, that the losses in one company can't be used to offset income in a different related-party company.

There should be no negative surprises to a Finder on April 15th.

Bad financial information typically leads to bad decision making.

If you expect to beat your competition, you must have better financial information infrastructure than does your competition.

Never borrow money from the IRS or any other governmental taxing authority.

Concentrate on your company's core competencies and avoid re-inventing the payroll and human resources wheels.

Use a payroll company to build your payroll and human resource infrastructure.

A company may be responsible for overtime, even if an employee is being paid a salary. The Department of Labor is powerful. Their laws, some of which were enacted in 1938, should be understood and complied with by the business owner.

A Finder should never relinquish control over the company.

Hostage-holding by one of your employees, whether voluntary or involuntary, is detrimental to any company.

A Finder should never allow an employee to hold the company hostage.

The Finder must understand the company's balance sheet.

Employee pay is dictated by the market.

An employee who is paid above market will eventually leave the company.

A Finder can't run the risk of not understanding the Statement of Cash Flows.

FROM CHAPTER 17

Finders create Triangular Relationships.

Co-owners should communicate with each other or end the relationship.

Finders are good at delegating responsibility but bad at giving authority.

Nepotism should be avoided at all costs. Family members should be treated like any other employee.

Family members should perform better for the company than regular employees. Family members should be fired if they perform below average.

There is never a win-win-win in a bad triangular relationship. The only permanent solution is to fix or remove oneself from such a situation.

FROM CHAPTER 18

Either you will outlive your company or your company will outlive you.

The less dependency upon key people, especially the owner, the more value will be assigned to a company upon an arms-length transaction sale.

The better the infrastructure, the higher the probability an owner has to increase a sales price of a company.

CHAPTER 20

My Favorite Quotes for Finders

It is lonely at the top is an aphorism that I mentioned in Chapter 2 of this book. Only those of us who are true Finders understand this statement. The following passage from James Allen's *As A Man Thinketh* lifts my spirits whenever I feel this loneliness. I wanted to give this pearl of great price its own chapter so it would stand out from the rest of the information in this book.

"The thoughtless, the ignorant, and the indolent, seeing only the apparent effects of things and not the things themselves, talk of luck, of fortune, and chance. Seeing a man grow rich, they say, 'How lucky he is!' Observing another become intellectual, they exclaim, 'How highly favored he is!' And noting the saintly character and wide influence of another, they remark, 'How chance aids him at every turn!'

"They do not see the trials and failures and struggles which these men have voluntarily encountered in order to gain their experience. They have no knowledge of the sacrifices they have made, of the undaunted efforts they have put forth, of the faith they have exercised, that they might overcome the apparently insurmountable, and realize the Vision of their heart. They do not know the darkness and the heartaches; they only see the light and joy, and call it 'luck'; do not see the long and arduous journey but only behold the pleasant goal, and call it 'good fortune'; do not understand the process, but only perceive the result and call it 'chance.'

"In all human affairs there are *efforts*, and there are *results*, and the strength of the effort is the measure of the result. Chance is not. 'Gifts,' powers, material, intellectual and spiritual possessions are the fruit of effort. They are thoughts completed, objects accomplished, visions realized.

"The Vision that you glorify in your mind, the Ideal that you enthrone in your heart – this you will build your life by, this you will become."

"Law, not confusion, is the dominating principle in the universe. Justice, not injustice, is the soul and substance of life. This being so, man has but to right himself to find that the universe is right; and during the process of putting himself right, he will find that as he alters his thoughts towards things and other people, things and other people will alter toward him."[27]

APPENDIX

A Word About B2B CFO®

Jerry L. Mills started a part-time CFO company in 1987. His intention was to be a sole practitioner in his business.

A couple of market conditions started changing in the late 1990s that caused Jerry to consider allowing other senior-level executives join his company. The first market shift was when closely held businesses started to accept the concept of a part-time CFO as their senior-level executive. The second market shift was an increasing supply of experienced professionals who were weary of working for one employer.

As market conditions changed, Jerry started allowing seasoned professionals to join his company. He formed a company named B2B CFO, LLC. He applied for and was subsequently awarded the trademarks for B2B CFO and Business-to-Business CFO. His firm has grown into a national company of seasoned CFOs.

The objective of the firm is to help improve infrastructure so the Finder can escape the trap of minding, as illustrated by the following:

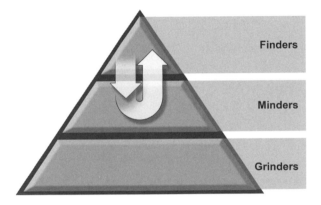

The firm has senior-level executives who help Finders get out of minding. The partners know how to build infrastructure so the Finders can get back to finding activities.

Each partner is supported by the combined intellectual knowledge of his or her fellow partners. They can communicate with each other, on a confidential basis, on a secured intranet environment.

It is highly unlikely that any Finder's company will have a need that the firm's partners can't meet.

Each partner has access to the latest GAAP, tax and other information via a secured intranet.

The partners do not require a contract for our consulting services. They work on a hand shake. All work is performed at the Finder's locations.

The firm's core values are:

- Honesty
- Integrity
- Objectivity

The firm's motto is: First direction, then velocity.

The partners have the skills necessary to help the Finder's company with its direction. One of the goals is to help build the company's infrastructure to help it achieve velocity.

The partners are listed on the www.b2bcfo.com.

Banking & Lending
Banking Relationships
Loan Packages
Capital Strategies

Financial Management
Train the Minders
Financial Statements
Projections
Budgeting

Cash Improvement
Working Capital Plans
Cash Forecasting
Experienced Advice

Profit Improvement
Financial Tools
Advice & Consultation
Gross Profit Analysis
Trend Analysis

B2B CFO®
FINANCIAL, STRATEGIC & TECHNOLOGY SOLUTIONS
Client Success

Exit Strategy
Value Improvement
Succession Planning
Sale of Business

Operations Improvement
Quality Control
Grinder Accountability
Management Training

Strategic & Business Planning
Business & Technology Alignment
Disaster Recovery Planning
Security, Reliability & Compliance

Sales Improvement
More Finding Time
Tools & Analysis

© 2007 B2B CFO®

NOTE REFERENCES

1. The Book of Positive Quotations, 494.
2. As a Man Thinketh, 50.
3. Built to Last, 11.
4. Ibid. 73.
5. Ibid. 74-75.
6. Good to Great, 195.
7. Built to Last, 9.
8. Ibid, 70.
9. As a Man Thinketh, 60.
10. Phrase taught to author by David Moore, Panamint Group.
11. The Millionaire Next Door, 240.
12. Business Finance, February 2006, 28.
13. Hibbingmn.com/dailytribune, Employee Theft on the rise, 3/20/2006.
14. Missoribusiness.net; The Problem with Employee Theft, 3/30/06.
15. Dictionary.com.
16. Britannica.com.
17. The Effective Entrepreneur, 99.
18. Success Through a Positive Mental Attitude, 155.
19. Intel.com.
20. Weopedia.com.
21. Quotations.home.worlnett.att.net.
22. Ibid.

23. Investopedia.com; EBITDA: The Good, The Bad, The Ugly, Feb. 2, 2002.

24. Dol.gov.

25. Ibid.

26. Metafilter.com.

27. As a Man Thinketh, 30, 56-57.